JOHN F. KENNEDY

Biography®

JOHN F. KENNEDY

Joyce Milton

LONDON, NEW YORK, MUNICH,
MELBOURNE, and DELHI

DK PUBLISHING
Publisher Chuck Lang
Creative Director Tina Vaughan
Editorial Director Chuck Wills
Art Director Dirk Kaufman
Production Manager Chris Avgherinos
DTP Designer Milos Orlovic

First American Edition, 2003
2 4 6 8 10 9 7 5 3 1
Published in the United States
by DK Publishing, Inc.
375 Hudson Street
New York, New York 10014

produced by AVALON PUBLISHING GROUP, INC.
Project Editor Max Alexander
Senior Director, Editorial Will Balliett
Senior Director, Operations f-stop Fitzgerald
Photo Editor Tracy Armstead
Designer Lisa Vaughn
Assistant Editor Kristen Couse
Production Manager Mike Walters
Production Editor Simon Sullivan

A&E TELEVISION NETWORK
Director of Licensing Carrie Trimmer
Director Legal & Business Affairs Chey Blake
VP/GM Consumer Products & Merchandising Steve Ronson

A&E and Biography are trademarks of A&E Television Networks.
All Rights Reserved © 2003 AETN

Jacket design copyright © 2003 A&E Television Networks
and DK Publishing, Inc.
Text copyright © 2002 Joyce Milton

Photo Credits—See page 152

DK Publishing, Inc. offers special discounts for bulk purchases for
sales promotions or premiums. Specific, large-quantity needs can
be met with special editions, including personalized covers,
excerpts of existing guides, and corporate imprints. For more
information, contact Special Markets Department, DK Publishing,
Inc., 375 Hudson Street, New York, NY 10014 Fax: 212-689-5254.

Cataloging-in-Publication data is available from
the Library of Congress

ISBN 0-7894-9316-0

Reproduced by ColourScan, Singapore.
Printed and bound by R.R. Donnelley in the United States.

See our complete product line at
www.dk.com

Contents

6
Preface: Unlikely Hero

8
A Dynasty in the Making 1849-1920

24
A Superior Sort of Summer Camp 1920-1934

38
Father vs. Son 1934-1940

52
Survival in the Solomons 1941-1946

70
Drafted into Politics 1945-1953

88
Author and Candidate 1954-1960

106
The Torch Is Passed 1961

120
A Leader Challenged 1962

132
Rendezvous with Death 1963

144
The Camelot Legacy 1963-1968

152
Photo Credits, Acknowledgements,
Index, Select Bibliography

Unlikely Hero

The Presidential election of 1960 was similar in many respects to the election of 2000: One of the major party candidates was a two-term Vice President. Although he was an experienced politician who had served under a popular Chief Executive, his personality was uninspiring and his speaking style so wooden that he reminded some observers of a marionette. The other candidate was the son of a famous father. More personable than his opponent, he benefited from an efficient campaign operation. Still, even some in his own party considered him too unseasoned to be president and suspected that his career so far owed less to talent than the energetic backing of his ambitious family.

On Election Day, the popular vote was almost evenly divided. The candidate with the famous name had garnered more electoral votes, but there were widespread charges of vote fraud, especially in one large state where the governor was a key supporter of the winner. Outraged supporters of the losing party complained that the election had been stolen. Others wondered if the outcome really mattered. Both of the candidates in the race had been centrists who agreed more than they disagreed on important issues. Moreover, despite an economy that had recently turned sluggish, it seemed likely that the new decade would continue the trends of the old, a time of expanding consumerism and social complacency.

When John F. Kennedy became the 35th president of the United States, no one predicted the crises and the tragedy that would mark his brief time in office. Personable and good-looking, Kennedy was a well-liked senator who had parlayed wartime heroism and two best-selling books into a presidential nomination, but his service in the Senate had been marked by a high rate of absenteeism. It seemed unlikely that anything he did as president would be as colorful or as controversial as the careers of his father and grandfather.

The Common Touch

For someone who grew up privileged and pampered, Kennedy (campaigning with Jackie for Senate re-election in East Boston, in 1958) relied on his wit and charm to connect with average voters.

A Dynasty in the Making
1849–1920

John Fitzgerald Kennedy was born on May 29, 1917, in the second-floor bedroom of a modest frame house at 83 Beals Street in Brookline, Massachusetts. He was the second son of Joe and Rose Kennedy, a young couple who, to all appearances, enjoyed a typical middle-class existence. Their nine-room frame house had been purchased for just over $6,400 and furnished on a budget. A live-in maid washed the baby's diapers in the kitchen, and during the winter months she often hung them to dry over the coal-fired stove. Rose also had help from a baby nurse. During John's infancy this post was filled by a woman named Kikoo Conboy, a recent immigrant from Ireland who spoke with a thick brogue and believed in the existence of leprechauns.

Perhaps the most notable thing about the Beals Street house was that it stood in a Protestant neighborhood. In the Boston area, Catholics and Protestants rarely mixed socially, and Catholics who insisted on crossing the invisible dividing line risked being thought of as pushy. But the Kennedys were no ordinary couple. Their wedding three years earlier had united two of Boston's most prominent Catholic families, and few doubted that the future would take them far from the petty social taboos that limited the ambitions of the "lace curtain" Irish, a group whose genteel manners and educational attainments separated them from compatriots still mired in the urban slums.

Young Rose

Although Rose Fitzgerald was an excellent student and athlete, her girlfriends were most impressed by her beautiful wardrobe. Rose's large hats were always in the latest style, and her clothes were decorated with elaborate hand embroidery and shirring.

The daughter of a two-term Boston mayor, Rose Fitzgerald Kennedy had studied languages and philosophy at a Sacred Heart convent school in Prussia. More than 450 guests attended Rose's lavish coming-out party in 1911, and she was immediately recognized as a leader of Catholic society. By the age of twenty she was already a member of the committee that evaluated children's books for the Boston Public Library, and she had organized a social club, the Ace of Clubs, for young Catholic women who had studied abroad and wanted to practice their conversational French.

Like other educated women of the day, Rose had been taught to view "household management" as an applied science. She kept a card file meticulously recording her children's doctor visits, illnesses, and other pertinent information. She closely watched the babies' food intake—just as she would later develop the habit of weighing all her own food on a portable scale—and she tried to keep them on a schedule, in accordance with the prevailing belief that regularity and order were essential to bringing up healthy children. Even though John and his older brother, Joe Jr., had a nursemaid, Rose took the babies out for a brisk walk in the fresh air every day. In the evenings, she played popular songs on the piano, and at bedtime, she read them stories or made up tales about episodes from American history or the Bible. A perfectionist with a deeply ingrained sense of religious duty, Rose attended early Mass every morning of her life and began taking the children to church as soon as they were old enough. If anything, she was a bit too conscious of the responsibilities of motherhood. Looking at her sleeping infants, she once said, she would be overcome by the knowledge that the smallest thing she said or did might affect their future, not just in the short run, but also "for all eternity."

Rose's husband, Joseph Patrick Kennedy, was a business prodigy who had achieved national attention in 1913 when he engineered the buyout of the Columbia Trust Company. Just 25 at the time, he was said to be the youngest bank president in the country, celebrated as something of a populist hero for saving a neighborhood "people's bank" from a hostile takeover. In 1917, the year of John's birth, Joe became the assistant manager of Bethlehem Steel's Fore River Shipyard. America's entry into World War I had placed heavy demands on the shipbuilding industry. Fore River was working at top speed, completing 36 naval destroyers in 27 months, including one that went from keel-laying to christening in just 46 days. Joe Kennedy was responsible for making sure that raw materials and parts arrived at the shipyard in time, and he was well rewarded for his efforts.

His salary was $20,000 a year, a magnificent sum in those days. But the job was unlikely to outlast the war, and Joe wasn't the type to spend windfall income. While he and Rose continued to live beneath their means, he was already making shrewd investments, laying the foundation for a fortune that would ensure his children's futures.

Joe Kennedy and his Fitzgerald in-laws didn't always get along, but they were united in having the highest expectations for the next generation. Joe had been bitterly disappointed at Harvard when not one of the seven exclusive clubs for undergraduates tapped him for membership. His determination to ensure that his sons would not have to suffer that kind of rejection was the driving force that pushed him into increasingly ambitious ventures. As he saw it, the factor that separated the Kennedys from the Boston Brahmins—the highly cultured, Yankee upper class—was the age of their money. It was his job to become wealthy so that the younger generation could acquire the cultural patina that would make them acceptable to the kind of people who belonged to Harvard clubs like Porcellian, AD, and Fly.

Rose's father, ex-mayor John F. "Honey Fitz" Fitzgerald, already saw a political dynasty in the making. When Rose gave birth to her first child, Joseph Patrick Kennedy, Jr., while vacationing at Nantasket Beach, the proud grandfather had entertained reporters who gathered outside the beach house by informing them that his new grandson would become president of the United States for "two or three terms." The reporters, who were used to Fitz's over-the-top rhetoric, had a good laugh.

The future of Joe and Rose's second son, the one named in the ex-mayor's honor, was as yet undecided. Jack, as he was called by the family, was a sickly toddler who had trouble keeping up with the active, adventuresome Joe Jr. It seemed that he was destined to be a typical second son, perpetually in the shadow of the firstborn.

Whatever Jack Kennedy might become in life, he was already part of a great American success story. The opportunities that lay before him were a long way from the desperation that drove his great-grandparents out of Ireland in the middle of the nineteenth century, in flight from a terrible famine estimated to have taken more than a million lives.

COFFIN SHIPS

An illustration from an English newspaper of 1850 shows Irish immigrants crowded together on the deck of a ship bound for America.

In the decade after 1845, a million and a half emigrants left Ireland for the United States. Another 340,000 sailed for ports in Canada, often to continue their journeys to the States by other means. Most of these emigrants were people of modest means who had sold their belongings to pay the fare—the equivalent of several years' wages. The rest were paupers, subsidized by sympathetic landlords or charitable organizations.

The heavy demand for trans-Atlantic berths led unscrupulous operators to sell passage on unseaworthy tubs. By 1849, the year JFK's great-grandfather Patrick Kennedy left the port of New Ross bound for Boston, the conditions on board a typical emigrant ship were deplorable. Passengers were jammed into the holds four to a bunk—an allotment of just eighteen inches of space per passenger. Food was moldy and scarce, the water foul. Many passengers were infected en route with "ship fever," or typhus, a disease spread by lice. Lengthy delays for repairs, quarantines and the captains' inability to post required bonds before entering U.S. ports were common. Infants, the elderly and the simply unlucky often could not survive such extended confinement. The "coffin ships" were well named.

The Irish immigrants who arrived in America during the decade that began in 1845 were usually not the poorest of the poor. Those unfortunates could not afford the fare and were more likely to perish from starvation. Because of oppressive laws passed by Ireland's British rulers, however, the famine immigrants usually lacked useful skills. They were also likely to arrive with young children and elderly dependents, a circumstance that limited their mobility. Within a few years inner city neighborhoods of American cities were filled with a population of recent arrivals who did not share the dominant religion or culture. Fairly or not, the newcomers developed a reputation for alcoholism, brawling and support for anti-British organizations like the Young Ireland movement. They often faced blatant discrimination, including signs that warned NO IRISH NEED APPLY. Nevertheless, despite alarmist predictions that the famine refugees would never assimilate, within fifty years a remarkable transformation had occurred. Nowhere was this more apparent than in the city of Boston. By 1900, the city had more Irish than Dublin, and Irish-American politicians dominated local government.

THE USUAL IRISH WAY OF DOING THINGS.

Anti-Irish

A cartoon by Thomas Nast combines two prevalent stereotypes of Irish-Americans, who were scorned as hard drinkers and political malcontents. The immediate inspiration for the drawing was an outbreak of fighting between Protestant and Catholic factions in New York in 1871. But Nast's litany of complaints also includes the Fenian Council, formed in America with the goal of supporting the violent overthrow of British rule in Ireland.

Patrick Kennedy, the great-grandfather of the future 35th president, was not in himself an immigrant success story. The younger son in a family of relatively prosperous tenant farmers, Patrick emigrated from Dunganstown in County Wexford in 1849 and found work in Boston as a cooper, making whiskey barrels for a distillery. In 1858, however, Patrick died of cholera, leaving behind a widow, Bridget, and four children. Bridget kept a small shop, selling needles and thread, and later worked as a hairdresser at the Jordan Marsh department store. Her only son, Patrick Joseph, quit school at 14 to work on the docks.

Life was hard for the Kennedys. Still, P.J., as he was called, managed to save and borrow enough money to become a partner in a rundown saloon on Border Street in East Boston. With his stocky build and walrus mustache, P.J. had the look of a bare-knuckle boxer, and he was said to have a mean streak when crossed. For the most part, however, he was a cautious businessman, whose idea of recreation was a quiet evening at home with a good book. P.J. sold liquor for a living but rarely drank it, and he was happily married to Mary Augusta Hickey, the sister of a police lieutenant. Mary was an intelligent, well-organized and ambitious woman, but perhaps her most

outstanding characteristic was her striking blue eyes. The "Hickey eyes" were a feature that she would pass on to her only surviving son, Joseph Patrick Kennedy and, through him, to many of his descendants.

Joe Kennedy, born in 1888, showed an early talent for making money—raising pigeons that he sold to local restaurants, where they appeared on menus as roast squab. Young Joe was an enigmatic combination of intense ambition and insecurity. He had a chip on his shoulder about being Irish, resented any hint of discrimination, and was quick to get into fights. It almost seemed that the generations had been reversed. P.J., who had spent his youth as a stevedore and a bartender, quietly transformed himself into a successful businessman, with holdings that included a wholesale liquor distributorship as well as coal mining and banking interests. His son, reared in a relatively affluent home by loving parents, would never quite shake off his crude manners and street-fighter mentality. And perhaps he didn't want to jettison them. These things were the visible badges of the anger that drove him to succeed.

Early in his career, P.J. had used his saloon to establish himself as the boss of Boston's Second Ward. In the days before entitlement programs, most government largesse was dispensed in the form of patronage, at the pleasure of the ward boss. It was a system that worked well for those who had the right connections and were willing to exchange loyalty for favors, though not well at all for everyone else. P.J. developed a reputation as an especially generous patron, one who would often dig into his own pocket to pay a hard-up customer's coal bill or cover the cost of a doctor's visit to a sick child. The Christmas baskets he distributed were the envy of those who had the bad luck to live outside his district. Loyal voters elected P.J. to the state legislature, and he eventually became Boston's wire commissioner, responsible for bringing electric lights to the city.

Mary Hickey Kennedy often complained that the constant stream of supplicants was a drain on her husband's finances, but this was a shortsighted way to look at the situation. Young Joe knew better. Like all ward bosses, he depended on "ward heelers," operatives who patrolled his district on foot, rounding up his loyal supporters for meetings and primary elections. If there weren't enough voters to be found, they resorted to other tactics. Once, Joe heard a couple of ward heelers boast to his dad, "Pat, we voted 128 times today." P.J.'s political career was supported by the liquor interests, who knew they could count on him to oppose temperance legislation, and he eventually became

Young Joe Kennedy
The ambitious Mary Hickey Kennedy was determined to transform her only surviving son into a gentleman. Among Joe's many childhood jobs was a stint as a stock boy for a haberdasher, but he always seemed ill-at-ease in fine clothes.

THE IRISH NORTH END

Before 1845 Boston was a homogenous city with few foreign-born residents. But the establishment of a Cunard Line terminal in 1841 helped make Boston the destination of choice for Irish immigrants, and by 1855 they made up fully a third of the population.

The earliest immigrants usually found their way to the neighborhood known as the North End. As middle-class families fled, their houses were taken over by slumlords who divided the spacious rooms with thin partitions, creating a warren of cramped apartments. Often, they also enclosed the front stoops to create additional living space

New arrivals from Ireland crowded into Boston's North End, transforming the historic neighborhood.

and built makeshift additions in the former backyards. Boston's toll bridges long discouraged immigrants from straying from their North End and East End neighborhoods, creating a divided city.

John Francis Fitzgerald, the 35th president's maternal grandfather, spent the first three years of his life in a typical North End tenement located at 30 Ferry Street, where his family was considered lucky to have an apartment with a window.

a member of the Boston Democratic party's five-man strategy board, which doled out patronage jobs and city government contracts. Political clout undoubtedly contributed to his growing fortune.

Next to being a saloonkeeper, running a grocery store was an ideal basis for political success in 19th-century Boston. In fact, the two paths often amounted to nearly the same thing. Groceries were allowed to sell liquor by the drink, and in the evening hours they often functioned as neighborhood social clubs where workingmen gathered to partake of a shot or two and mull over the news of the day. John F. Kennedy's maternal relatives, the Fitzgeralds, owed their rise to the grocery business founded by Thomas Fitzgerald and his brother James.

Thomas and his wife Rosanna married in 1857, the same year the family grocery store opened. They began their family while living in a typical slum tenement in Boston's heavily Irish North End. Within a few years, however,

they were prosperous enough to become landlords themselves, purchasing a three-story brick house at 435 Hanover Street. The growing Fitzgerald brood occupied the two lower floors while no fewer than four families of renters shared the top floor.

Tom and Rosanna would have twelve children in all, three of whom died in infancy. In 1879 Rosanna was pregnant for the thirteenth time when she heard that an excursion train carrying her husband and nine boys to a church picnic had been involved in a terrible accident. The shock caused her to suffer a stroke, and she was dead before word came that the rumor was untrue. There had been no train wreck.

Of all the Fitzgerald offspring, the fourth son, John Francis, was outstanding. Born in 1863, he was a short, feisty lad who made a name for himself by winning footraces and swimming competitions. When it came time for high school, he won entrance to Boston Latin, a competitive public school where boys of all ethnic backgrounds applied themselves to a rigorous classical curriculum. Johnny learned to translate Virgil, memorized vast swaths of English poetry and studied the orations of William Pitt and Daniel Webster. On his high school graduation, he was accepted directly into Harvard Medical School.

Johnny's dream of becoming a doctor ended abruptly a year later with the death of his father. Rather than see his five younger brothers parceled out to relatives, he made up his mind to quit medical school and care for them. For the next several years, Johnny became both mother and father to his orphaned siblings. He washed dishes, scrubbed floors and saw to it that all the boys were neatly dressed for school. In need of an income, he appealed for help to Matthew Keany, the boss of the Sixth Ward, who agreed to take him on as a protégé. Starting from a patronage job as a Customs House clerk, he succeeded Keany as ward boss, earning the nickname "Honey Fitz" from the flow of syrupy oratory that issued from his lips. In 1894 he was elected to Congress, becoming the only Roman Catholic in the House of Representatives at the time.

Honey Fitz retired from the House after three terms, and in 1905 he was elected mayor for the first time. From taking care of five orphans, he had graduated to a new role as the surrogate father of the "dearos"—all those who hailed from the "dear old North End." His schedule was filled with dinnertime strategy meetings, charity committees,

Honey Fitz's Last Hurrah

Always quick to adopt innovations, Honey Fitz toured the city in an open motorcar during his 1905 race for mayor of Boston. By 1922, when he ran for governor, the hyperactive Fitz had become a parody of himself, and his habit of delivering orations and songs from the backseat of a touring car was considered risible. Fitz suffered a humiliating loss, ending his career in elective politics.

HONEY FITZ

Honey Fitz and Joe Kennedy were often at odds, but they shared the dream that a member of the younger generation would become the first Catholic president.

John F. Fitzgerald, who was mayor of Boston from 1906 to 1907 and from 1910 to 1914, owed his nickname "Honey Fitz" to the honeyed oratory that flowed from his tongue. Fitz, it was said, had a repertoire of jokes and anecdotes that could wring a smile from the corpse at a wake. He was a master of the "Irish switch," which consisted of chatting up one voter while shaking the hand of another, and his speeches segued smoothly from bellowed denunciations of "the bosses" to sentimental evocations of County Mayo (where he had never lived) and disquisitions on the fine art of catching fish.

When he ran out of words, Fitz would close his campaign rallies by singing for the crowd, usually his signature tune, "Sweet Adeline." Once during a rally, he was knocked down by an out-of-control truck. While rescuers struggled to free his leg from under a wheel, Fitz kept on singing, determined to reassure the crowd that he was all right. Friends affectionately referred to Fitzgerald's speaking style as "Fitzblarney." But not everyone was amused. As a popular ditty of the time put it, "Honey Fitz can talk you blind/on any subject you can find." He died in 1950 at the age of 87, having had the satisfaction of seeing his grandson elected to Congress.

banquets, weddings and wakes, not to mention ball games, picnics, ship christenings and dances. Nothing made him happier than attending two or three functions in a single evening, and a Boston newspaper estimated that he had made 3,000 speeches in his first two years as mayor.

Whether or not it was really true that politics was a drain on the Kennedy family fortune, this certainly couldn't be said of the Fitzgeralds. Honey Fitz soon had his entire family on the city payroll, including one brother whose sole duty was to pick up the daily traffic report from the Warren Street toll bridge and deliver it to city hall. Fitz thought of himself as an upright man, and he emerged relatively unscathed from a major bribery scandal that broke during his administration. Still, the Fitzgeralds seemed to live remarkably well considering Fitz's modest income.

Inconveniently enough, the extroverted Honey Fitz had married a reserved, semi-reclusive woman who loathed politics. Tall, slender and highly aware of her own dignity, Josie Hannon was Fitz's second cousin and his first sweetheart. Josie wanted nothing to do with public life, and for a number of years she even refused to live in her husband's House district, insisting on a home in Concord, where she could cultivate her passion for horseback riding.

Having lost his only two sisters in their infancy, Honey Fitz was delighted when his and Josie's first child turned out to be a girl. He doted on Rose

The Fitzgerald Family
The popular mayor of Boston poses with his dignified, rather humorless wife, Josie, and their children. Standing, left to right, are Mary Agnes, Thomas, John Francis Jr., and Rose. Eunice is seated at right, and the baby of the family, Fred, born in 1904, stands between his parents.

Elizabeth, born in 1890, and she remained very much his favorite even as the family grew to include two more girls and three sons. Rose never took her position for granted, however, especially after the age of seven, when she heard President William McKinley describe her five-year-old sister Agnes as "the prettiest girl ever to come into the White House." Brunette, blue-eyed Rose was pretty in her own right, but she strove to please her father by using her mind. Aside from his outgoing personality and addiction to the sound of his own voice, Fitz's most notable trait was his intellectual curiosity, and Rose did her best to keep up with her father's wide-ranging interests. When he gave a speech in Congress advocating higher immigration quotas, she researched the subject too, and defended the same position in a high school debate. An A student, she became at fifteen the youngest person ever to graduate from Dorchester High School.

Even though she emulated her father, Rose had a great deal of the haughty Josie Hannon in her. A stickler for propriety, she once lectured her sister Agnes for being seen outdoors eating bread and molasses—hardly, in Rose's opinion, a dignified meal for the mayor's daughter. On another occasion, finding herself on the trolley without a penny in her purse, she introduced herself to the motorman, confident that her name alone would earn her a free ride, courtesy of the city. (And it did.) Like her mother, Rose was clothes-proud. Her beautifully tailored shirtwaists and coats and, especially, a velvet hat trimmed with an ostrich plume, were the envy of her friends.

Whether it was because of her outgoing, confident personality or her stylish clothes, Rose caught the eye of young Joe Kennedy, just two years her senior. With his red-gold hair, dazzling white teeth, and those penetrating blue "Hickey eyes," P.J.'s son cut a dashing figure. He was also an outstanding athlete, and in 1907 he won the Mayor's Cup as the best school league baseball player in the city. If Rose was an Irish-American princess, Joe was a princeling.

He somehow got admitted to Boston Latin, where his grades hovered between Ds and Fs and he was forced to repeat his junior year. Though no student, Joe was popular enough to be elected president of his senior class, and the school yearbook cheerfully predicted that he would make his living "in a very roundabout way." Despite his poor grades, he was accepted by Harvard, no doubt thanks to his father's influence.

Sixteen-year-old Rose and eighteen-year-old Joe, fell in love at Old Orchard Beach, Maine, where their families had gone for summer vacation. It seemed unlikely that anything would come of this holiday romance. Fitz and Josie considered their daughter too young for a serious courtship, and she had her heart set on attending Wellesley, the elite women's college. However, a few days before her freshman year was to begin, Rose was shocked

"Sweet Adeline"

Even at an advanced age, Honey Fitz never missed an opportunity to entertain. Though strongly identified with "Sweet Adeline," a song Rose taught him, he had a large repertoire of sentimental ballads.

OLD ORCHARD BEACH

Teenage romance flourished under the watchful eyes of family and friends. Posing on the beach, sixteen-year-old Rose Fitzgerald, at right, is flanked by her future father-in-law and her brother John. Joe Kennedy, 18, is second from the right. These summer vacations at public resorts in Maine and Massachusetts formed the model for later Kennedy clan gatherings, at the family's private compound in Hyannis Port.

By the end of the nineteenth century, Old Orchard Beach in Maine had become the favorite vacation spot of Boston's "high Irish" families. The oceanfront strand of gingerbread hotels and rambling "cottages" offered an escape from the August heat, but hardly much of a change of pace. The same families who socialized together in the city were reunited at big hotels like the Brunswick, where matrons relaxed on the porch in the cool evening air while their husbands played cards inside.

As busy as any Boston street, the beach was lined with a jumble of cafes, concession stands, shooting galleries, and rental carriages. Children gravitated toward the boardwalk, which boasted a merry-go-round and other amusements.

Boston Brahmins looked down their noses at the raffish atmosphere, but for regulars it was a magical place. Many a couple fell in love while strolling along the busy beachfront, among them Joe Kennedy and Rose Fitzgerald.

A Quiet Wedding

Joe and Rose leave the home of the archbishop of Boston, William Cardinal O'Connell, after being married in his private chapel (right). Only 75 guests attended the wedding breakfast, an intimate gathering by Fitzgerald standards.

Playing to Win

Joe was a fierce competitor who took athletics seriously. As captain of the Boston Latin high school baseball team, he had a .667 batting average, and (below) during his summer vacations from Harvard, he played semipro ball.

to learn that her father had changed his mind about her education after the Archbishop of Boston chided him for setting a bad example by sending his daughter to attend a Protestant-run institution. With his administration plagued by charges of corruption, Fitz couldn't afford to offend Boston's most prominent Catholic leader. And so Rose, much to her dismay, became a student at the Sacred Heart Convent in Boston, where the curriculum included such unfamiliar subjects as medieval history and needlework.

A year later, Fitz and Josie decided to send Rose and Agnes abroad to attend another Sacred Heart convent school in Blumenthal, Prussia. At this elite institution, students were expected to speak German and French when they were allowed to speak at all, and to follow a rigorous schedule that began at 6 AM. Agnes found the convent cold and unfriendly, but Rose, to her own surprise, had never been happier. The quality of the religious education, the Gregorian chants, the exposure to masterpieces of religious art and architecture, the total immersion in a self-contained world with its own rules and values, all awakened a contemplative side of her nature whose existence no one, least of all she herself, had suspected. In a letter home, Rose teased her parents by observing that she was becoming "extremely angelic." She began to rise even earlier than the other girls to spend extra time at prayer. At the end of the year she was chosen for membership in the elite sodality known as Les Enfants de Marie, the Children of Mary. Membership entitled Rose to use the initials E.D.M. after her name for the rest of her life. In turn, she vowed to model herself after the Immaculate Mother, attending Mass daily and practicing "a certain habit of mortification" as well as the virtues of "kindness, gift of self-abnegation [and] evenness."

After spending an additional year at another Sacred Heart convent in New York, the future Manhattanville College, Rose returned to Boston to become her father's unofficial hostess and advisor. She hadn't forgotten about Joe Kennedy, whose picture she had hidden in her suitcase during her year abroad. But Honey Fitz was now utterly opposed to the match. It isn't clear exactly why he didn't want his favorite daughter to marry Joe Kennedy. This is one of those topics that Rose would later cover with a veil of selective amnesia. Nevertheless, Fitz tried everything he could think of to keep the young couple apart, including whisking Rose away for a vacation in Palm Beach, Florida, an extended tour of Europe, and a junket to Panama, where Fitz inspected the operations of the Canal and somehow left Panamanians with the impression that "Sweet Adeline" was the national anthem of the United States. When in Boston, Rose sneaked off to see Joe in secret, wearing a black veil over her face so that they wouldn't be recognized while ice skating together on Scarboro Pond.

Rose might never have gotten up the courage to defy her beloved father if it weren't for the "Toodles" affair. In 1913, the pugnacious James Michael Curley, who was opposing Fitz's bid for a third term as mayor, threatened to make an issue of a report that Fitz had been seen kissing and hugging one Elizabeth "Toodles" Ryan, a cigarette girl, in a private dining room of a restaurant-*cum*-gambling den known as the Ferncroft Inn. Even by the standards of 1913, Toodlesgate was hardly a major scandal. But Josie was

distraught and humiliated, and Fitz's image as an ideal family man was shattered. Rather than subject his family to further embarrassment, Honey Fitz withdrew from the race. Although Rose sympathized with her father, she was no longer quite so afraid of his disapproval. She and Joe were married a year later, on October 7, 1914.

Honey Fitz tried to revive his political fortunes. In 1918 he was elected to Congress, only to become the target of a House inquiry, which determined that his victory was the result of fraud. A number of the decisive ballots for Fitzgerald had been cast in the name of voters previously killed in combat in World War I. Others were "mattress votes," cast by individuals who lived outside the district but registered at local bars or brothels. The House refused to seat Fitzgerald, awarding the district to his opponent, Peter Tague. All of Fitz's campaign tactics had been used before in Boston politics, and doubtless would be used again. But the era when the ward bosses settled their differences privately in rooms redolent with cigar smoke was over. As long as James Michael Curley was in power, there was no chance that his popular rival would be allowed to regain any measure of influence. The once beloved Honey Fitz would henceforth be portrayed in the press as a crook and a buffoon.

The year 1918 also saw the first cracks in the façade of Joe and Rose's model marriage. With the war winding down, Joe left the Fore River Shipyard to join the Boston office of the Hayden, Stone and Company brokerage house. New to the stock market, Joe soon earned a reputation as a shrewd and nimble speculator. Many of the tactics he employed were considered unsavory, though in a largely unregulated market they were technically legal and by no means uncommon. He was a master of market pool, an operation similar to the "pump and dump" tactics of more recent times. A group of investors would begin to trade a company's stock among themselves, creating the impression of heavy demand for the shares. When other investors piled in, driving the price up even farther, the members of the pool sold out at a tidy profit. Joe's new job involved frequent trips to New York, and Rose began to suspect that his absences weren't all business-related. Probably she was correct. It seems that Joe had occasional dalliances with chorus girls throughout the time that he was courting Rose, which may have been the source of Honey Fitz's doubts about him.

The little house in Brookline was beginning to feel like a prison to Rose.

A Perfect Family

The arrival of her third child marked the high point of Rose's dream of rearing an ideal family. Joe Jr., left, was a sturdy boy, but Jack, right, suffered a string of childhood illnesses and had trouble keeping his weight up. Meanwhile, Rosemary, center, failed to attain developmental milestones. For several years, doctors dismissed Rose's concerns about her daughter as the imaginings of an overanxious mother.

In September 1918, when Jack was sixteen months old, Rose gave birth to her third child, Rosemary. By the following summer, she was pregnant again, but her marriage was in serious jeopardy. From Joe's point of view, the problem was sex, or rather the lack of it at home. Rose took literally the Catholic teaching that sexual intercourse was permissible only for the purpose of procreation. Among other things, this meant that marital relations were forbidden during pregnancy, and Rose was usually pregnant. Under the circumstances, Joe felt he had a good excuse for straying from his vows.

In an otherwise strong marriage, Rose might have been tempted to rethink her views on sex. As she saw it, however, she had been relegated to a corner of her husband's busy life. Joe's stock manipulations depended on absolute secrecy, and he made it a rule never to discuss business at home. Nor did he get involved with the problems of the children. This, as he put it, was his wife's "department." When Joe was at home he was often distracted and moody. Rose later told the story of the winter day when her husband went out for a walk, pulling Joe Jr. behind him in a sled, and became so engrossed in his own train of thought that he failed to notice that the toddler had fallen off the sled and into a snow bank.

Rose was used to the companionship of her father, a compulsive talker who had sought her advice regularly. It's little wonder that she had trouble adjusting to a mate who never confided in her. She had made no close friends among her Protestant neighbors, and even the Ace of Clubs was turning out to be a disappointment. The other clubwomen quickly lost interest in speaking French and studying world affairs, preferring to plan "pink teas" and charity benefits.

Even Rose's confidence in her abilities as a mother was being sorely tested. In an era when it was considered important for babies to do everything on schedule, Joe Jr. had met every benchmark with ease. But Jack was a different story. Chronically underweight, he had to be coaxed to eat, and caught every bug that came along. And Rosemary, a beautiful, healthy baby at birth, also seemed to be developing slowly.

In January 1920, Rose decided that she couldn't go on any longer. Packing a suitcase, she moved back home to her parents' house, where she spent the better part of three weeks in her old bed, napping the day away. At last, Honey Fitz came to her bedside and told his daughter she couldn't go on this way. "You've made your commitment, Rosie, and you must honor it now," he said. "What is past is past. The old days are gone." It was up to her to figure out a way to make the marriage work, Fitz went on. If she needed more time to herself, then so be it.

Rose took the advice to heart. She was eight months pregnant with her fourth child and she couldn't resign from motherhood even if she sometimes wanted to. Rose returned to the house on Beals Street, but the Kennedy marriage was about to change in ways that would have profound consequences on the children, especially young Jack.

Rose's Card File

Rose acquired the habit of keeping a card file from her father, who meticulously recorded every favor he did for his constituents, from patronage appointments to free holiday turkeys. In her own file, she kept track of her children's doctors' visits and illnesses, a lengthy chronicle in Jack's case.

A Superior Sort of Summer Camp

1920–1934

Surprisingly enough, Rose did manage to ease some of the burdens of family life onto her husband's shoulders. Soon after she returned home from her father's house, two-and-a-half-year-old Jack was stricken with scarlet fever, a highly contagious and, at the time, often fatal disease. Rose was expecting to give birth at any moment, so the task of keeping watch beside Jack's bed at Boston City Hospital fell to his father. It was the first time someone Joe loved had been seriously ill, and the experience affected him deeply. In a letter thanking the doctor for his "wonderful work" in saving his son, Joe wrote, "During the darkest days I felt that nothing else mattered except his recovery."

Nevertheless, once Jack was well enough to leave the hospital, he was shipped off to Poland Springs, Maine, to recuperate in the care of a nurse. This would be the pattern throughout Jack Kennedy's childhood and teenage years. His health remained precarious, but there was usually some other family situation, such as the birth of another baby, that prevented his parents from being at his bedside to comfort him.

Kathleen Kennedy, born during Jack's illness, would rarely give her parents anything to worry about. Active, adventuresome, and cheerful, "Kick" became the family's golden girl, universally popular with adults and her peers. Rosemary, on the other hand, was breaking her mother's heart. Slow to walk and talk, she grew into a little girl who could not handle a knife and fork, balance

JOE KENNEDY, BOOTLEGGER

Beer kegs were emptied into the gutters on the day the United States officially banned the sale of alcoholic beverages.

Beginning in 1920, the Volstead Act prohibited the manufacture or sale of "intoxicating liquors" anywhere in the United States. Ironically, the coming of Prohibition only made the Kennedy family's liquor importing business more profitable. Joe Kennedy continued to purchase Scotch whisky and Caribbean rum through his connections abroad. The liquor was offloaded from ships onto "rum rows," deserted beaches on the eastern end of Long Island, where it was picked up by associates of gangster Frank Costello. Cases of brand-name spirits, sometimes diluted up to 50 percent with water, were then resold to high-end speakeasies and wealthy private customers.

Rose Kennedy always insisted that she had no idea what business her husband was engaged in, but in other circles Joe's lucrative but illegal sideline was an open secret. His reputation as a bootlegger with mob connections made him socially unacceptable in some circles, but there were exceptions: In 1922 Joe volunteered to provide the liquor for the tenth reunion of his Harvard class, a gesture that was gratefully accepted.

herself on a bicycle or steer a sled. Doctors assured Rose that she was just being an over-anxious mother; Rosemary would catch up to the other children in time. A few years later they changed their minds, pronounced Rosemary mentally retarded, and declared that nothing could be done to help her. Wealthy families in the 1920s usually placed such children in institutions or with a sympathetic couple, but Rose made a valiant effort to integrate Rosemary into the life of the family.

Rose later acknowledged that in her preoccupation with Rosemary, Jack often got short shrift. Frequently confined to bed with bronchitis or some childhood malady, Jack loved being read to. Although the task was often delegated to a nanny, Rose did her best to steer Jack toward good literature, beginning with tales of King Arthur and his Knights of the Round Table and moving on to classics like *Treasure Island* and *The Jungle Book*.

In the fall of 1920 the Kennedys moved to a house in a more upscale section of Brookline, one large enough to accommodate their growing family and an even faster growing staff of domestic helpers. Rose and Joe now had separate bedrooms, though this didn't prevent Rose from getting pregnant almost immediately. Eunice, the third Kennedy daughter, was born in July 1921.

By the time they were eight and six years old, respectively, Joe Jr. and Jack were enrolled at the Devotion School, a public grade school named in honor of Brookline resident Edward Devotion. Joe was a sturdy boy who attacked life head-on, while Jack had already learned to rely on his winsome charm. But despite their very different personalities, the boys were accomplices in mischief. Rose's diary from this period records her rueful enjoyment of boys' pranks and Jack's precocious wit. One evening, following a day at school and a visit with family friends, Jack startled her by remarking, "Well, here I have been home only a few hours and already the cops are chasing me." Inquiring further, Rose learned that Jack had been teasing one of the neighborhood girls. When the little girl complained to a passing policeman, Jack escaped a lecture by running away and hiding in a cellar.

About six weeks later, the boys saw a sign that read NO DOGS ALLOWED IN THIS RESTAURANT and altered it to read NO HOT DOGS ALLOWED... Two days after that, with Halloween approaching, they stole some false mustaches from a neighborhood shop. And in December Jack warned Rose that his teacher would soon be paying her a call. Offering his excuses in advance, he explained that he was doing all right in class, but "if you study too much, you're liable to go crazy."

For the most part, Joe seemed to have accepted his increased domestic responsibilities with good humor, and Rose was getting into the habit of treating herself to vacations from the cares of motherhood. In 1923, she and her sister Agnes departed on a six-week tour of the western United States. Joe sent her telegrams filled with cheerful and reassuring news about the children. "I hope you are having a real good time because you richly deserve it," he wrote. "Please do not think too much about us and spoil your party." But Joe's newfound dedication to family did not last long. When his sixth child, Patricia, was born in May 1924, he was busy in New York stanching a raid on the shares of John Hertz's Yellow Cab Company, and a month went by before he could get home to see the new baby.

By this time, Jack and Joe Jr. were fast developing into neighborhood terrors, and their parents transferred them to the Noble and Greenough

The Scamp

Sandwiched between a highly competitive older brother and a succession of sisters, Jack fell into the role of the lovable underachiever who relied on his sense of humor to get by. Here, dressed for the beach, he sits still long enough to have his picture taken with a tickled Rosemary, an uncharacteristically pensive Kathleen, and the perpetually worried Eunice.

THE KENNEDY COMPOUND

After being rejected by the Cohasset Country Club, Joe Kennedy decided to make his summer base in Hyannis Port where, he was assured, the local club would admit him. In 1925, he rented the so-called Malcolm Cottage, actually a good-sized clapboard house dating from 1902, which stood on two and a half acres and had its own private beach.

Three years later Kennedy purchased the property and hired Boston architect Frank Paine to do a major renovation. Paine doubled the size of the house to 14 rooms and 9 bathrooms, enough to accommodate a large and still growing family. Over the years, the Kennedys acquired adjacent properties as they came on the market.

An aerial view of the Kennedy Compound from 1960 shows the main house (3), as well as a neighboring "cottage" that had been purchased by Robert and Ethel Kennedy (2) and a house belonging to Jack and Jackie (1). Tennis courts (4) and a helicopter landing site (5) occupied part of the original lawn.

John and Jackie bought a large house next-door to the original "cottage" in 1956, and another neighboring house was purchased by Bobby and Ethel Kennedy.

By the time it was added to the National Register of Historic Places in 1960, the Kennedy Compound had grown to 60 acres. Although many sightseers set out to visit the compound, it is fenced and guarded, and can best be glimpsed from the water.

School, a private academy whose students included such scions of the Boston aristocracy as future national security advisor McGeorge Bundy and Leverett Saltonstall, Jr., the son of a rising power in the Massachusetts Republican party. The Kennedy boys were apparently the only Irish Catholics there, and when arguments broke out, the other children taunted them for being "micks." Joe reacted by getting into fights at recess, but such insults seemed to slide right by Jack. Noble and Greenough's principal, Myra Fiske, became the first of many teachers to conclude that Jack was smarter than his older brother, but his abilities would rarely be reflected in his grades. Joe was a dutiful student who did reasonably well in everything. Jack applied himself only when a subject piqued his interest.

Joe Kennedy very much wanted his children to take their places among America's social and political elite, but his efforts to make this possible were constantly frustrated by his own notoriety. Aside from his reputation as a stock manipulator, he was heavily rumored to be in partnership with the mob, profiting from the sale of smuggled liquor to speakeasies. When the lower school was in danger of closing, Joe organized a committee of parents to repurchase the building from a developer who was planning to tear it down. But despite leadership in the campaign to save the school, he and Rose were still not invited to the homes of the other parents. Embittered, he concluded that Yankee Boston would always see him as an outsider, and that his children would never be entirely accepted either.

Around this time, Joe began to think about becoming a movie mogul. In the entertainment business, it didn't matter if your ancestors hadn't arrived in 1620 on the *Mayflower.* Moreover, since it was hardly unknown for producers to turn to the mob for financing, Joe's associations with bootleggers would do him no harm. In 1926, after lengthy negotiations, he put together a group of investors to purchase the Film Booking Office of America. FBO, as it was called, was primarily a distribution company, though it also owned a Hollywood studio that turned out profitable low-budget westerns featuring box office favorites like Tom Mix. It was an era of consolidation in the movie industry, and Kennedy was able to follow this acquisition with a series of deals that put him in control of the Keith-Albee and Orpheum theater chains. In 1928, he structured the merger of FBO and Keith-Albee-Orpheum with RCA, creating the industry giant RKO. RKO included the venerable Pathé, the company that produced the first movie newsreels in 1910. Pathé stockholders were outraged to find that under the terms of the buyout their stock was valued at only $1.50 a share, while those of Joe Kennedy and his group of insiders were worth $80.

Young Jack Kennedy's popularity at school soared when the guests at his tenth birthday party were treated to a private showing of Tom Mix westerns from his dad's studio, projected onto a movie screen in the Kennedy living room. But Jack was seeing little of his father, who divided his time between Hollywood and FBO's main office in New York City. There were now seven Kennedy children, including a third son, Robert Francis, born in November

MOVIE MILESTONE

August 3, 1926
Warner Brothers and Vitaphone presented the first public showing of a motion picture with a sound track. *Don Juan,* starring John Barrymore, was not technically a "talking picture," since it had sound effects and music, but no dialogue.

Hyannis Port

With Joe and Rose often traveling and the older children beginning to go off to boarding schools, summers at Hyannis Port took on the characteristics of a family reunion. Sharing a joyous moment during the summer of 1931 are, left to right, Bobby, Jack, Rosemary, Jean, Joe Sr., Rose, Pat, Kathleen, Joe Jr. and Eunice. Ted, named for Joe's longtime friend and aide Edward Moore, would make his appearance the following year.

1925, and Rose was reluctant to uproot the family and move to a strange city. In the fall of 1927, she finally agreed to come to New York, where the Kennedys rented a spacious house in the Riverdale section of the Bronx. Homesick and pregnant again, Rose almost immediately left the children in New York in the care of nursemaids and went home to her parents' house to await the arrival of her fifth daughter, Jean, in February 1928.

The Kennedys soon moved again, this time to a Georgian home on five acres of land off Pondfield Road in Bronxville, an upper-class enclave in the Westchester County suburbs. Joe also purchased the rambling frame house in Hyannis Port that the family had previously rented for their summer holidays on Cape Cod. Reminiscences by and about the Kennedys have a great deal to say about Hyannis Port, but curiously little about the house on Pondfield Road. Perhaps this is because the family was seldom together there. Almost as soon as his wife and children joined him in New York, Joe began a tumultuous affair with film star Gloria Swanson. When not in Hollywood with Gloria, where he kept a house on Rodeo Drive, Joe was often vacationing in Palm Beach, Florida. Rose also spent a good deal of time in Palm Beach and made numerous trips to Paris, where she invariably stayed in

the same room in the Ritz Hotel, shopped for couturier clothes and took private French lessons in a vain attempt to exorcise her American accent.

In the fall of 1929, Joe Jr. became a boarding student at the Choate Preparatory School, and Rosemary was sent off to a convent school soon after. Jack, the only one of the older children left at home, was delivered to the Riverdale Country Day School in a chauffeur-driven Rolls-Royce. An ever-changing corps of governesses, nannies, tutors, cooks and housekeepers supervised him and his younger siblings.

From his first meeting with Gloria Swanson in November 1927, Joe Kennedy was mesmerized. The movies' reigning femme fatale, famous for her heavy-lidded eyes and dangerous-looking teeth, was the first Hollywood star to dress her servants in full livery and the first to marry a title, taking as her third husband the Marquis de la Falaise de Coudraye, known in Hollywood as Hank Falaise. She was also the first movie star to bear a child, daring to challenge the prevailing belief that the public would never accept a mother in romantic roles. A sexually liberated woman who had formed her own company to produce a movie version of Somerset Maugham's steamy novel *Rain,* Gloria was very much Joe's female counterpart—a high-stakes player in business and in life. Less enamored than her lover, Swanson took note of Joe's badly cut suits and his utter lack of artistic taste. Still, he had a rough-hewn physical vitality and was generally acknowledged to be a financial genius. He confidently promised to relieve her of all her worries, finding a way to shepherd her version of *Rain* past the industry censorship board and straightening out her problems with the IRS, which was challenging her contention that all her clothes, jewels, and makeup—the costs of being Gloria—ought to be deductible business expenses. She soon signed a power of attorney that gave him a free hand to fire her most trusted employees, streamline her company, and manage her finances as he saw fit.

In the past, Joe's affairs had been reasonably discreet. This time, he was so eager to flaunt the relationship that it is hard to avoid the conclusion that he was deliberately trying to provoke Rose into leaving him. He invited Gloria to Hyannis Port, where she made a deep impression on Jack by arriving in a seaplane. And in August 1929, he booked her on the same crossing of the *Ile de France* on which he, Rose, and his sister Margaret Burke were traveling to Europe.

By this time, the affair was common gossip, and according to some accounts Honey Fitz had already urged his daughter to deliver an ultimatum to Joe. Nevertheless, Rose pretended to be oblivious, going out of her way to be gracious to her husband's "business associate." Her position was that she

Gloria Swanson

During the course of their three-year affair, Swanson complained, Joe took control of her independent film company and her personal staff. He even persuaded her to change her adopted son Joseph's name to Joseph Patrick. While Hollywood gossips traded anecdotes about the temperamental lovers, Rose insisted that her husband and Swanson were just "business associates," prompting Swanson to wonder if Rose was a better actress than she was.

QUEEN KELLY

Swanson, at 29, played a naive schoolgirl swept off her feet by a Prussian nobleman in *Queen Kelly*.

Joe Kennedy's affair with Gloria Swanson was the impetus for *Queen Kelly*, one of the legendary disasters in the annals of Hollywood. The improbable plot featured the ultra-sophisticated Swanson in the role of a sixteen-year-old student at a Sacred Heart convent school who captures the attention of a passing prince by flinging her underpants at him.

Kennedy, a novice producer, envisioned a melodrama of epic proportions and hired the notoriously temperamental director Erich von Stroheim—who overspent his budget and shot thousands of feet of unusable film. Some key scenes were so lewd that there was no hope of getting the picture into American theaters. The film was seen only in Europe, in a version cobbled together after von Stroheim was fired.

American audiences got a glimpse of the lost film in 1950, when footage was incorporated into *Sunset Boulevard*, which featured Swanson as a faded movie queen clinging to memories of her glorious past, and von Stroheim as her enigmatic butler.

was the wife, and her husband's occasional flings were beneath her notice.

In truth, Rose did not have many options. As a devout Catholic, she could never agree to a divorce. Nor was a legal separation a reasonable option. Given Joe's need for control, Rose would surely have spent the rest of her life as a supplicant, dependent on Joe's good humor for financial support and access to the children. Rose also had no desire to subject her children to the bitterness she had witnessed at home during the Toodles affair. Simply ignoring Gloria and hoping her husband's grand passion would wear itself out probably seemed the sensible course of action.

And, indeed, Swanson was already on her way out. Joe's enthusiasm for the affair seemed to cool in tandem with his ambition to make movies. He was a man who couldn't tolerate failure, a dysfunctional trait in a movie producer. As Swanson saw it, however, what really doomed their relationship was Joe's inability to tolerate a lover who wasn't afraid to challenge his judgment. One of their first blow-ups occurred when Swanson tried to talk Joe into sending Rosemary to see her personal diet doctor. Ahead of her time, Swanson believed that most human ailments were the result of consuming "poisons" like red meat, and she thought a regimen of raw vegetables might cure Rosemary's mental retardation. Kennedy, quite understandably, told her to mind her own business. He had taken his daughter to the best specialists on the East Coast, and he wasn't about to subject the girl to the whims of a Hollywood food faddist.

More serious trouble arose after Gloria learned that a new Cadillac Joe had given one of her directors as a bonus had actually been charged to her account. Checking her company's books, she discovered that she had also paid for the magnificent fur coat Joe gave her as a gift as well as numerous other "presents." When her accountants finally unraveled Gloria Films' complicated contractual arrangements with Joe Kennedy, they concluded that Swanson had paid for the disastrous film *Queen Kelly*, while Joe had taken the tax loss.

By 1930, the Swanson affair was history. Rose, it seemed, had triumphed, and the birth of the Kennedys' ninth and final child, Edward, followed in 1932.

But victory came at a price. Sexual indiscretions became Joe's vehicle for expressing his suppressed anger at Rose and his free-floating frustrations with the world in general. His behavior grew more flagrant and more embarrassing as the years went by. He was seen in New York and Palm Beach nightspots in the company of glamorous models, on occasion fondling the women in full view of embarrassed customers at nearby tables. He hugged and pinched his daughters' teenage friends and, as his sons grew older, made a habit of propositioning their dates. To an amazing degree, the Kennedy children came to see such goatish behavior as normal, or at least to be expected, and they learned to make excuses for it.

At the same time, the children thought of their mother as weak and powerless, and they assumed that this, too, was the general rule. The strain of trying to ignore the obvious gradually transformed Rose into an emotionally withdrawn woman who lived in psychological denial. When staying at Hyannis Port, Rose played nine holes of golf in the morning, toting her own clubs to avoid the necessity of making small talk with a caddy. In the afternoons, she took long walks on the beach, or retreated to a tiny prefabricated dressing room with a view of the shore, where she could read undisturbed for hours.

There were so many subjects that Rose chose to ignore that it became increasingly difficult to have a conversation with her. A compulsive note-writer, Rose communicated with her children by leaving notes on their pillows. She was also an early practitioner of the group letter. Each of the children would receive a copy of the same compilation of news and motherly advice. Thus, Jack would be privy to his mother's opinion that Jean needed to watch her weight and stop helping herself from the bread plate, while Jean, presumably, read all about Jack's losing battle with Latin. Knowing that anything one told Mother would be broadcast to all the siblings in her next group letter undoubtedly discouraged the children from confiding anything too personal.

Jack was old enough to recall a time when his mother had been warm and caring, and he found her descent into denial especially painful. At times, he sympathized and wanted to defend her, but he also resented her emotional paralysis and self-absorption. "My mother is a nothing," he once told a friend.

A Handsome Couple

Though living largely separate lives, Joe and Rose were always careful to cultivate the appearance of a happily married couple. She ignored Joe's philandering, including the presence of his longtime mistress, Janet Des Rosiers, who was hired as Joe's "secretary." The children largely accepted the situation, and Jack later found a job for Des Rosiers at the U.S. embassy in Paris.

The children's feelings toward their father were much more complicated. Joe Kennedy's glaring flaws make it easy to forget that he could also be very charming and genuinely affectionate. Joe's letters to his children were deeply supportive, and he never dispensed boilerplate advice. He knew each child's strengths and weaknesses and, apparently, was well informed about their schoolwork and problems of the moment. Even his lectures were delivered in the context of assurances aimed at propping up the child's confidence in his or her ability to do much better.

On a day-to-day basis, however, the atmosphere that Joe created in his household was that of a superior sort of summer camp, one where he functioned as camp director and head coach. Even at Hyannis Port, when both parents were in residence, the children's days were supervised by a team of hired hands, starting with morning calisthenics on the lawn under the direction of a full-time physical education tutor. Joe valued promptness and Rose was a stickler for good table manners, but unlike in many large families, there was little emphasis on neatness or responsibility to the household. Rose occasionally made fitful efforts to teach the children the meaning of hard work, organizing berry-picking expeditions or sending the boys off to dig clams, but she was too distracted to supervise regular chores. Young Bobby once signed up to deliver newspapers in Bronxville, but his father ended that experiment when he learned that Bobby had enlisted the chauffeur to cover the route in the family Rolls-Royce.

The real assignment of every Kennedy child was to compete and win. Unlike Rose, who tried to encourage her children to read, Joe thought it was unnatural for children to sit around indoors. He entered them in swimming races when they were as young as six or seven. By the time the children reached their teens, the focus shifted to sailing. Just doing one's best wasn't enough. Joe drummed into the children the lesson that winning was everything, and he was vocally disappointed with anything less than first place. In the absence of other challenges, the Kennedys organized their famous touch football games on the lawn. Summer houseguests, including on occasion pregnant women, were expected to take part, and they were

All Work and No Play. . .
Jack Kennedy never outgrew his passion for competitive sports. Here, during a visit to Hyannis Port in 1952, he takes a break from plotting strategy to play softball with members of his staff.

ridiculed by the Kennedy kids if they appeared not to be playing hard enough.

Even dinnertime was another competitive occasion. After the age of six, the children were expected to eat with the adults and come to the table prepared to hold their own in conversation—typically by posing questions about world affairs to their father.

This focus on winning undoubtedly built character and taught the children to set high goals for themselves. In another family a child like Jack, who was underweight and often ill, might have been assigned the role of the cosseted invalid. Instead, Jack learned to persevere without complaint and use his natural wit to compensate for a lack of physical stamina.

Still, even the children themselves came to recognize that the emphasis on winning for Team Kennedy was overdone. "I was twenty-four years old before I learned that I didn't have to win something every day," the youngest daughter, Jean, once said. Around Hyannis Port the Kennedy kids developed a reputation for being sore losers, and there were persistent rumors that their sailboats were illegally rigged with extra sail.

Competitiveness untempered by good sportsmanship eventually led the children to have unrealistic confidence in their abilities. More than one Hyannis Port guest has observed that despite their spirited play, the Kennedys were not really very good at touch football. Visitors simply figured out that it was impolitic to beat the family at its favorite game. One family friend, who put his advice in the form of a set of "Rules for Visiting the Kennedys," advised, "To become really popular you must show raw guts…Laugh off twisted ankles or a big hole torn in your best suit. They like this. It shows you take the game as seriously as they do. But remember. Don't be too good."

No matter how entertaining a guest might be, he always had to keep in mind that he was still an outsider. The Kennedys were constantly exchanging compliments, and reporting on compliments that other people had paid to members of the family. Honest but helpful criticism from others was not appreciated. As the author of "Rules for Visiting the Kennedys" further noted, "Anticipate that each Kennedy will ask you what you think of another

THE SAILOR

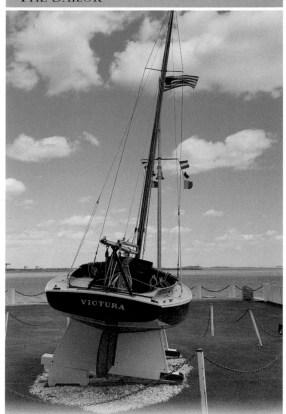

The *Victura*, on display at the John F. Kennedy Library.

An avid sailor from childhood, Jack Kennedy won two sailing trophies as a teenager in his own boat, the *Victura*, a gift from his parents on his fifteenth birthday. The 26-foot sloop was a Wianno Senior class boat, manufactured in 1932 at the Crosby Yacht Yard in Osterville, Massachusetts. When Jack went away to college, the *Victura* remained at Hyannis Port, where he sailed it almost daily when he returned to the Cape during summer vacations. In 1944, a hurricane struck Cape Cod, damaging the Kennedys' house, but Jack managed to save his boat by securing it at its pier. Later, he used the sloop to teach Jackie how to sail, and enjoyed both solitary and family outings after he entered the White House. As his friend Dave Powers recalled, "If the President wasn't sailing on *Victura* he was thinking about it, as evidenced by his many doodles of the sailboat."

Jack and Lem

Accustomed to competing for attention at home, and regularly chauffeured to and from his various schools, Jack seems to have had no close friends until he began rooming with Lem Billings at Choate. Lem was an outsider from a modest background. A closeted homosexual, he could be trusted to keep a secret, and he was one of the few people privy to the details of Jack's health problems.

Kennedy's a) dress, b) hairdo, c) backhand, d) latest public achievement. Be sure to answer 'Terrific.'"

Joe had planned for his two oldest sons to attend Choate, the elite prep school for boys located in Wallingford, Connecticut. But for some reason, when it came Jack's turn in the fall of 1930, he was sent to Canterbury, a Catholic school in New Milford, Connecticut. Perhaps Joe thought Jack wasn't mature enough for Choate and would benefit from a trial run at Canterbury, where classes were smaller and the boys received more individual attention.

Even so, Jack had a tough time. All fall he was dreadfully homesick, and by late winter he had come down with a fever of 105 and a bad case of hives. "The icheting is ferocious," he wrote his mother in a letter replete with fractured spelling. His eyesight was deteriorating, he complained, and "everything is a blur at over eight feet." Moreover, the school doctor was worried about Jack's inability to keep his weight up. In an effort to get the 13-year-old above 105 pounds, the doctor had prescribed a tonic. Jack reported that his special diet "results in recieving some kidding about my delicay [sic]" from his fellow students. That spring Jack fainted during chapel, and over Easter vacation the family physician decided to remove his appendix. Jack didn't recover well from the surgery, and he never returned to Canterbury.

In spite of this troubling experience, Jack spent the summer cramming in enough Latin to erase a failing grade, and the following September he joined Joe Jr. at Choate. Too impulsive and disorganized to make any progress in his studies, Jack was soon failing French as well as Latin, and his French teacher despaired that he inevitably showed up in class without his textbook, paper, or a pen. He wanted desperately to be a football star like his brother Joe, but in addition to being scrawny, he had a weak lower back, described by one doctor as a congenitally "unstable" spine. Chronically late and untidy, he came to blows with his roommate over his sloppy habits.

During his second year at Choate, Jack was assigned a new roommate, a doctor's son from Pittsburgh named K. LeMoyne Billings. Lem idolized the more charismatic, witty Jack, and with the benefit of an appreciative audience, Jack blossomed into the class jester.

He organized practical jokes in the dorm and soon excelled at the smutty patter so delightful to adolescents. In class, he managed to derail his teachers' most carefully crafted lesson plans by asking irrelevant questions. Through it all, the Choate faculty demonstrated an admirable patience. As the headmaster, George St. John, wrote in a letter to Mr. Kennedy, Jack had "a clever, individualist mind," and it was never easy to harness independent thinkers.

Considering the state of Jack's health, the headmaster had reason to cut his difficult pupil some slack. During his first year at Choate, Jack was confined to the infirmary in November and again in February, troubled by swollen glands that may or may not have been mumps. In his second year, February once again saw Jack bedridden, this time with what appeared to be flu. The same pattern held in his third year. This time, however, Jack was so ill that he was transferred to a hospital in New Haven for observation, where he suffered another outbreak of the hives that plagued him at Canterbury.

As infuriating as he could be when well, Jack was a gallant and endearing patient. He entertained himself by reading serious biographies and English history, including Winston Churchill's *The World Crisis.* And no matter how miserable he might be, he made an effort to put his visitors at ease with jokes and wisecracks. Jack became a favorite of the nurses, and the headmaster's wife appointed herself his surrogate mother, stopping in to see him whenever possible. Amazingly, Jack's parents never came to visit.

When he became well enough to travel, Jack was sent down to Palm Beach to spend the rest of the winter term at the oceanfront house that his father had recently purchased from department store magnate Rodman Wanamaker. He returned to Choate after Easter to finish his fifth form (junior) year, and then was shipped off to the Mayo Clinic in Rochester, Minnesota. For a full month, world-class diagnosticians poked and prodded Jack, prescribed multiple enemas, and used a foot-long metal tube to explore his colon. It was a frightening and humiliating ordeal for a boy who had just passed his seventeenth birthday. In a letter to Lem, filled with the usual adolescent obscenities and boasting, Jack confided that even his sex drive was minimal. In the family's version of Jack's biography, this illness would be written off as hepatitis. In fact, the doctors didn't know what was wrong with Jack, and they were equally mystified by his sudden recovery. By August, he would be in Hyannis Port with the rest of the family, competing successfully in sailing races.

Winston Churchill
Often bedridden, Jack used his enforced leisure to devour volumes on English and American history. One of his favorite authors was Winston Churchill, who extolled British traditions of political liberty and advocated a strong response to the rising power of Nazi Germany. Jack's avid reading marked the difference between him and his older brother. While Jack's views on world affairs were already starting to evolve, Joe Jr. would cling to their father's isolationist position.

Father vs. Son
1934–1940

Some time before his affair with Gloria Swanson ended, Joe Kennedy had recognized the signs of a top-heavy stock market and cashed out most of his holdings in the motion picture business. He began to sell stocks short, and the Wall Street crash of October 1929 left him better off than before. Jack, a student at Canterbury at the time, heard nothing about the market's plunge until the subject came up in class. In the years that followed, Joe occasionally alluded to the country's economic troubles when lecturing Jack about running up excessive bills for incidentals like getting his suits pressed. But the Kennedy children were never affected in any significant way by the Great Depression, which would become the formative experience for so many of their contemporaries.

During the 1930s, Joe's interests shifted toward politics. An early supporter of Franklin Delano Roosevelt, Joe raised funds for his 1932 campaign at a time when the business community was hardly enthusiastic about the Democratic candidate. Perhaps his goal was to pave the way for his eldest son. But some of Joe's friends, including *New York Times* columnist Arthur Krock, were convinced that Joe saw a chance to become president himself. In an era when presidential candidates were still chosen in smoke-filled rooms, it was conceivable that a political neophyte with a large bank account could eventually become the standard-bearer of Democrats disenchanted with the FDR's leadership.

Scotland's Pride – the World's Choice!

DEWAR'S "White Label" SCOTCH WHISKY

Scotch Whisky is the finest drink in the world

Whiskey Baron

Through his company Somerset Importers, Joe was a major importer of Scotch whiskey. Over the years, Somerset was often accused of unfair business practices. Wholesalers complained that in order to get premium brands like Dewar's White Label, they were forced to purchase many cases of cheap rum from a distillery, in which Joe had a financial interest. During the late 1930s, when it was feared that war would soon cut off supplies, Joe was accused of hoarding Scotch to drive up the price.

Joe hadn't entirely lost interest in making money. In 1933, with the end of Prohibition imminent, he traveled to England with James Roosevelt, where his very public friendship with the president's son helped him to secure an exclusive contract with United Distillers, the distributor of Haig & Haig and Dewar's scotch, among other premium brands.

Joe's immediate goal was a place in Roosevelt's cabinet, preferably as secretary of the Treasury. Instead, in 1934 he was offered the chairmanship of the newly established Securities and Exchange Commission, empowered to curb abuses like insider trading and stock pools—the very market strategies that had made the Kennedys rich. In a typical response, *The New Republic* called Joe's appointment "grotesque." From a practical standpoint, however, Roosevelt had made a smart move. If Joe Kennedy said that Wall Street could live with the new federal regulations, other brokers would find it awkward to take issue with him.

While his father grappled with the problems of drafting regulations for the stock market, Jack entered the sixth form, his final year at Choate. Surprisingly fit, he set out to instigate rebellion. Several months into the year, he found his inspiration when George St. John gave a talk urging his charges not to become "muckers," his term for the kind of boy who muddles through life without benefit of uplifting goals or values. The word's similarity to a certain Anglo-Saxon obscenity was irresistible to Jack and Lem. They promptly formed a Muckers Club whose members met in secret to swap irreverent song lyrics and plan anarchistic pranks that rarely got beyond the fantasy stage. The thirteen Muckers even went so far as to order custom-made gold pins in the shape of their club logo, a shovel.

For the long-suffering headmaster, whose family had gone out of its way to be kind to Jack when he was ill, this was a declaration of war. George St. John decided to expel Jack, then changed his mind, only to get hot all over again after the school intercepted a cheeky telegram from Kick Kennedy, addressing Jack and Lem as "Dear public enemies one and two." Doubtless it never occurred to Jack that St. John might take the Muckers rebellion personally. To his adolescent mind, Choate represented the epitome of adult hypocrisy in general and Establishment snobbery in particular.

Playing the instigator was a way for Jack to distinguish himself from his older brother. Despite an average IQ and a somewhat overbearing personality, Joe had distinguished himself in football and on his graduation was awarded

the Harvard Prize, bestowed annually on the student who best exemplified the qualities of the scholar-athlete. Jack was lucky to graduate at all, though he scored a last-minute coup by getting himself elected as the senior "most likely to succeed." Far from being an unsolicited testimonial from his peers, the outcome of the vote was Jack's final prank, accomplished through energetic politicking and vote trading.

An enthusiastic capitalist in practice, Joe Senior knew that most intellectuals at the time believed that the future lay with socialism. Hedging his bets, he had arranged for Joe Jr. to spend a year in England between Choate and Harvard, studying at the London School of Economics under the renowned left-wing economist Harold Laski. According to the entry for John F. Kennedy that would later appear in *Who's Who*, Jack also spent the year after his Choate graduation studying with Laski. In fact, Jack registered in October and withdrew a month later, apparently on account of illness. Returning to America, he belatedly joined the freshman class at Princeton, where Lem Billings and other friends from Choate were enrolled. By December Princeton, too, was a washout. Jack was forced to withdraw and enter Brigham Hospital in Boston, where doctors were once again mystified by his gastric upsets and plummeting white blood count. He finished the 1935-6 school year at a ranch in Arizona that offered plain food and outdoor labor to patients recuperating from serious illnesses.

The regimen worked so well that in the fall of 1936 Jack was able to get a fresh start on college, entering Harvard as a freshman. Heedless of his fragile health, he went out for the swim team, specializing in the backstroke, and played freshman football. Loading up on ice cream and steak, he even managed to get his weight up to 160 pounds. Torbert Macdonald, a football coach's son who would become Jack's best friend at Harvard as well as captain of the Crimson eleven, was impressed by Jack's grit and courage, but even his coaching could not make the skinny freshman into a first-team player. A year later, while practicing with the junior varsity, Jack wrenched his "unstable" back, ending his career in Harvard athletics.

As at Choate, Jack sometimes struggled with academics but had no difficulty making friends.

JFK AND ADDISON'S DISEASE

Jack's thin build, bronzed complexion and auburn hair made him highly photogenic. Ironically, these very qualities were markers for Addison's disease.

The mysterious ailments that plagued JFK throughout his youth and early adulthood finally made sense when he was diagnosed with Addison's disease, a rare endocrine disorder characterized by the failure of the adrenal glands to produce enough of the hormone cortisol. Addison's symptoms include weight loss, fatigue, and low blood pressure. The skin may also take on a brownish tint. If early warning signs fail to lead to a proper diagnosis and treatment, the patient goes on to suffer what is known as an Addisonian crisis, characterized by a severe pain in the lower back and/or abdomen, vomiting, and diarrhea.

Since adrenal hormones help the body fight off infections, surgery can be dangerous for Addison's patients unless they are given a course of injections before the procedure to raise their cortisol levels. Jack was very fortunate to survive the back operations he underwent before the nature of his illness became known.

With the support of two buddies, who vowed to reject any bid that did not include Jack, he even became the first Kennedy accepted into one of Harvard's elite clubs, a distinction that eluded his brother Joe. Girls were drawn to Jack's boyish looks; guys found him an entertaining companion whose wit could put an amusing spin on whatever happened to be going on at the moment. Only a few of Jack's closest friends were aware that he lived with chronic pain, and probably none of them knew what he really felt about anything. He was uncomfortable with raw emotion, preferring the light, bantering tone of the young sophisticate.

At home, Jack had a different image. His love of reading and developing interest in current affairs marked him as the family intellectual, possibly with a future in journalism or even as a history professor. So far, however, his academic career had been anything but sterling. When not held back by illness, Jack was hampered by his refusal to take himself seriously. He was perpetually late, much to the annoyance of his father, and usually inappropriately dressed when he did show up—the kind of kid who found it a challenge to put together a matching pair of socks.

After his freshman year, Jack looked forward to a summer in Hyannis Port devoted to sailing, working on his tan and pursuing girls. Instead, Joe talked his son into making a tour of Europe. It was 1937 and, given the unsettled political situation on the Continent, there was no telling how long such travel would be possible. Lem Billings, who had lost his father a few years earlier, borrowed money from the Kennedys so that he could afford to make the trip with Jack. Lem was determined to travel cheaply, a goal complicated by Jack's decision to take along his own car, a 1936 Ford convertible. The sight of two American college boys rich enough to ship a large, shiny automobile across the Atlantic inevitably inspired innkeepers to raise their rates, a situation Jack thought quite unfair.

Jack and Lem did their best to live up to their image of dissolute youth, Ivy League style. They were kicked out of several *pensions* for having girls in their rooms, and managed to bluff their way into a gambling club in Monte Carlo, despite being under the legal age. Always ready with a quip, Jack observed that his command of French was improving although the only thing French about Lem was his bad breath.

When not looking for dates, they also crammed in a full schedule of sightseeing, and more. Like so many young Americans at the time, Jack and Lem had fantasies of getting across the border into Spain where they could cover the ongoing civil war as freelance journalists. Unlike many of his Ivy League contemporaries, however, Jack favored the Catholic nationalist forces

Traveling in Style

When Jack went to Europe during his 1937 summer vacation, he took his new Ford convertible with him. His traveling companion, Lem Billings, snapped this photo of the Ford being unloaded from the deck of the transatlantic liner SS *Washington* onto the pier at Le Havre. Despite having the car, they considered themselves to be traveling on a budget.

of General Franco. Fortunately, no doubt, he and Lem failed to make their way across the border and had to be content with listening to the stories of refugees in the cafes of St. Jean-de-Luz. Arriving in Rome well prepared with letters of introduction, they had a private audience with Cardinal Eugenio Pacelli, the future Pope Pius XII. They also met Count Galeazzi, a powerful Catholic lay leader, who invited them to dinner and lectured them on the benefits of fascism.

Jack was prepared to listen to arguments in favor of fascist economics, which had provided Italian workers with a safety net of benefits similar to the programs Roosevelt was advocating in the U.S. Still, it was impossible not to notice the regimentation of Italian life and the ubiquitous propaganda. Posters of Mussolini were everywhere. Italy, however, was placid compared to Germany. Trying to gauge the mood of the country, Jack and Lem picked up hitchhiking students and even got into a long conversation with an English-speaking storm trooper in the Munich Hofbrau House. But the young people they met were almost invariably unpleasant and aggressively anti-American. Unlike his brother Joe, who was rather favorably impressed when he visited Germany in 1934, Jack was filled with foreboding.

The trip ended in Britain, where Jack fell ill with the usual gastric upsets and hives. For once, he recovered quickly, and he and Lem were able to cap off their European tour with a stay at the Scottish manor house of Sir James Calder, the owner of the Haig & Haig distillery. By day, they consumed magnificent meals, went fly fishing and tramped around the countryside hunting grouse. Promptly at ten PM, however, their wealthy but frugal host shut off all the electric lights, leaving them stumbling in the darkness as they tried to make their way through a warren of hallways to the mansion's only bathroom.

Four months after Jack's return to Harvard, his father became America's ambassador to the Court of St. James. Even more than Joe Kennedy's appointment to head the SEC, the decision to send him to London stunned FDR's supporters. It could be understood only as a ploy to get a potential rival for the 1940 presidential nomination safely out of the country. Joe sailed for England in March 1938, where he was soon joined by Rose and his seven younger children. Only Jack and Joe Jr., both studying at Harvard, were left behind. The British press was enthralled by the novelty of an Irish-American ambassador who had sired nine children and made a point of refusing to wear

Canine Hitchhiker

During their meanderings through the Low Countries, Jack and Lem acquired a pet dachshund. Unfortunately, Jack had an allergic reaction to their new friend. An attack of asthma, followed by hives, forced him to give away the dog. He was still ill when he and Lem reached London. There a doctor blamed Jack's miserable state on his diet of chocolates and tomato juice.

THE KENNEDYS AT THE COURT OF ST. JAMES

Joe Kennedy once confided to a friend that his only purpose in becoming an ambassador was to get his family into the Social Register. While this was hardly the whole story, the 1938 presentation of his eldest daughters, Rosemary and Kathleen, to King George VI and Queen Elizabeth was sweet revenge for the rejections Kennedy had suffered at the hands of Boston society. An invitation to Buckingham Palace surely trumped any event along Boston's trendy Commonwealth Avenue. Coming out during the London Season was considered the epitome of social success for any American debutante.

The girls' debuts were even more of a coup for Rose. As her daughters' sponsor at Court, Rose was invited to tea by the queen as well as the mothers of all the British

On May 4, 1939, Ambassador Kennedy and his family sat for a formal photographic portrait before dining with the king and queen. Jack, on leave from Harvard for an independent study project, was present on this occasion.

debs who would be making their first appearances at court on the same day. On the day of the presentation ceremony, Rose also managed to outshine her daughters with her eye-catching attire. Her outfit, as described by biographer Gail Cameron, consisted of "an exquisite Molyneux gown, embroidered with silver and gold paillettes and court train of silver lame bordered with sequin bands," worn with a ruby and diamond tiara and ostrich plume fan. In 1961 Rose, who had not gained a pound in twenty-three years, wore the same gown to her son Jack's Inaugural Ball.

knee breeches at court. Joe also got approving notices in America when he announced that he was ending the "undemocratic" tradition of selecting an elite group of American debutantes for presentation to the king and queen. As it turned out, however, this egalitarian gesture did not extend to Kathleen and Rosemary Kennedy, who were eligible to appear at court as daughters of the American ambassador and could now make their London debuts without competition from other American girls.

Rosemary's participation in "the Season"—invariably capitalized to distinguish it from less important social seasons elsewhere in the world—was perfunctory, but Jack's favorite sister, Kathleen, soon emerged as the reigning belle of the moment. With her deep-set eyes, prominent chin, and odd figure—her large head and broad shoulders rested on an unusually short torso—Kick Kennedy could not be considered beautiful, but her winning personality more than made up for her physical limitations. London's smart set was just discovering American swing music, and Kathleen epitomized the same spirit of refreshing spontaneity. Playing to the hilt the role of the innocent American, the fun-loving Kick cheerfully accepted being teased about her ignorance of British upper-class manners, but always made sure that she gave as good as she got.

Perhaps because Kathleen was only eighteen at the time, it didn't seem to occur to Rose that her daughter's social triumph would inevitably lead to her falling in love with a British aristocrat, as firmly committed to Protestantism as the Kennedys were to the Roman Catholic church. Sure enough, Kathleen soon became attracted to Billy Cavendish, the Marquess of Hartington and heir to the Duke of Devonshire. The Cavendish family's strong ties to the Church of England went back to Henry VIII, who had bestowed on their ancestor lands seized from Catholic monasteries. Romantic and headstrong, Kathleen found it hard to imagine that in the mid-twentieth century religious differences still mattered enough to stand in the way of her happiness.

While fashionable London was taking Kathleen to its heart, the British public was growing disenchanted with her parents. Judging by Rose's memoirs, her time as hostess of the American embassy was one of the high points of her life. She seemed unaware that her showy couturier wardrobe and schoolgirl notions of gentility made her a ridiculous figure in the eyes of the aristocrats she hoped to impress. Joe, meanwhile, had become associated with the so-called Cliveden set, a group

Kick

Eighteen-year-old Kick's combination of girlish high spirits and quick wit made her an instant success in London society. Used to juggling several suitors at once, Kick fell hard for the aristocratic Billy Hartington, whom she met at a garden party in the summer of 1938. Hartington's background was so impeccable that he was mentioned as a possible match for the future queen Elizabeth II.

of politicians loosely gathered around the American-born member of Parliament, Lady Nancy Astor. The Cliveden set had a reputation for anti-Semitism, and they made the mistake of imagining that Adolf Hitler was a rational statesman. Since it would obviously be folly for Germany to fight a two-front war, they believed that the Third Reich would be amenable to a negotiated settlement of its claims to territories in Europe. Presumably, German Nazis and Soviet Communists would then wear each other down in a lengthy war of attrition.

Joe's belief that standing up to Hitler would be disastrous for Britain was reinforced by his 1938 meeting at Cliveden, Lady Astor's country house, with Col. Charles Lindbergh, who had recently made a tour of German air bases. Powerfully impressed by Germany's advanced aircraft and well-trained pilots, Lindbergh predicted that if war broke out the Luftwaffe would bomb England at will. Civilians, he thought, would never stand for months of air raids. In the end, England would be forced to sue for peace.

Such ideas reinforced Joe's own isolationist sentiments. The belief that the United States should avoid involvement in the quarrels of European nations had a long history going back to George Washington, and it could reasonably be argued that America's violation of this principle during World War I—billed as "the war to end all wars"—had only set the stage for a second, even more destructive conflict. Anti-interventionist sentiment flourished in its traditional strongholds in the American South and Midwest, but also among the descendants of Irish and Central European immigrants, who saw no reason to risk their lives to save the British Empire.

In the belief that he was more in tune with the sentiments of the average American than Roosevelt's State Department, the ambassador soon made a series of statements, both public and private, that undermined U.S. foreign policy and sent exactly the wrong signals to the Germans. He encouraged the British prime minister, Neville Chamberlain, in his policy of appeasement, and in a speech at a Trafalgar Day banquet he predicted that democracies and dictatorships would have to learn to coexist and work together at "solving their common problems." In a meeting with the German ambassador to England, Herbert von Dirksen, Kennedy groused that European leaders would never say anything positive about the Third Reich because they were "afraid of the Jews." The problem, he suggested, was not so much that Germany wanted to rid itself of Jews but that it made such a "loud clamor" about it.

Von Dirksen's account of this conversation would be published in 1951, sealing Joe Kennedy's reputation as an anti-Semite. The ambassador certainly had all the prejudices of his time; however, it would be more accurate to say that he didn't care about the Jews one way or the other. Nor did he care about the Czechs, the Poles, the French or, in the long run, the British.

"Peace in Our Time"

British prime minister Neville Chamberlain waves to a cheering German crowd after agreeing to Hitler's demands for the dismemberment of Czechoslovakia. Joe Kennedy supported Chamberlain's strategy of placating Hitler in the hope of averting all-out war. But Chamberlain's hope that Nazi Germany would take a long time to digest its new acquisitions proved hollow. A year later, the Germans invaded Poland.

All of these peoples were just annoying obstacles in the way of his goal of keeping America out of war. Lacking any deep understanding of world politics, he simply could not see how the domination of Europe by a totalitarian regime would have any appreciable impact on life in the United States.

While the name of Kennedy was becoming indelibly associated with appeasement in the minds of the British public, Joe did his sons the dubious favor of getting them involved in his diplomatic mission. Joe Jr. graduated from Harvard in 1938 and became his father's personal secretary in London. The following year, Jack made arrangements to spend the spring semester of his junior year doing an independent study project in Europe. Traveling with a letter of introduction from Secretary of State Cordell Hull, Jack made his way through Europe, the Middle East, and the Soviet Union. With Europe edging ever closer to war, harried American Foreign Service officers were none too pleased to learn that they were expected to conduct impromptu tutorials for a Harvard undergraduate who was ostensibly on a "fact-finding" mission for his father—the same Joe Kennedy who refused to listen to the advice of the State Department. Despite this well-justified resentment, Jack certainly benefited from the opportunity to observe the European situation firsthand. The lengthy letters he sent to his father in London were the work of a young man who was beginning to acquire a grasp of the nuances of international relations, the very quality his father lacked.

After spending some time in London, Jack returned to the Continent in the summer, accompanied by his Harvard roommate Torby Macdonald.

Fact-Finding

By the summer of 1939, Joe Jr. was working in the U.S. embassy in London while Jack, 22, was conducting an unofficial fact-finding mission on the Continent. Meanwhile, the British Foreign Office had opened a secret file to collect reports of pro-German statements made by the Ambassador, and President Roosevelt was irate over his unstinting support for Chamberlain.

Torpedoed at Sea

Passengers are rescued from the liner *Athenia* after spending anxious hours adrift in lifeboats. Jack, sent to Glasgow to reassure the American survivors, was confronted by a frightened and hostile group that had little faith in the American ambassador or the protective power of the Neutrality Laws.

In Munich they joined up with Byron "Whizzer" White, the all-American football player and future Supreme Court Justice. While touring the city in a borrowed car, the trio came upon a street demonstration and stopped out of curiosity. According to Jack's joshing account, the demonstrators appeared to be singing about a Nazi hero named "Worst Hessel" (actually, Horst Wessel). Some storm troopers on the scene soon noticed their car's English license plate and began throwing bricks. Jack and his friends made a narrow escape.

Undeterred by this experience, Jack finished off his independent study with a visit to Czechoslovakia. The Czech government was already under Nazi control, and the country's borders were closed to tourists. The skeleton staff left at the American embassy was astounded to learn that Ambassador Kennedy's son was arriving to put the finishing touches on his Harvard independent study project. With difficulty, they figured out an excuse to get him through the German lines and arranged for him to interview various Czech notables.

August 20, 1939, found Jack in Berlin. He still wasn't sure there would be a war—the Germans he met seemed to think that England would back down once again and let them take Poland. But the U.S. chargé d'affaires knew

differently. He gave Jack a message to carry to his father, predicting that war would break out within a week.

On September 1, Germany invaded Poland. Two days later, Great Britain declared war, and Londoners began anxiously searching the skies, looking for the first signs of Luftwaffe bombers. At the American embassy, Joe Kennedy ordered the construction of a bomb shelter, and he and his staff began fielding requests from thousands of frantic Americans who wanted to book passage home. On the morning of September 4, the embassy received a report that the *Athenia*, a British liner carrying 1,400 passengers bound for Canada, had been torpedoed and sunk by German submarines. Unable to get away from London, the ambassador sent Jack to Glasgow to meet with the American survivors.

Accompanied by his father's personal assistant, Eddie Moore, Jack brought the survivors a message that a U.S. flag vessel, immune from attack by virtue of American neutrality, was being dispatched to take them home to the United States. The traumatized Americans were not at all reassured by this news—understandably, since a German U-boat commander had apparently mistaken the *Athenia* for a British naval vessel.

"We want a convoy!" they shouted. One woman loudly pointed out that the entire U.S. Navy had scoured the Pacific for the missing aviatrix Amelia Earhart and wondered why their safety didn't merit the same level of concern.

Jack handled the situation as gracefully as possible, but he couldn't erase the general feeling that the ambassador had insulted the survivors by sending a boy to do a man's job. British newspapers described the youthful-looking Jack as a "schoolboy," variously giving his age as eighteen or nineteen. In fact, he was 22.

Returning to Harvard a few weeks later, Jack found the campus bitterly divided over Roosevelt's plan to sell armaments to Britain on favorable terms. Like his father, he still hoped that the president would be able to broker a peaceful settlement of the European situation. On the other hand, he greatly admired Winston Churchill, and during the course of the school year he grew increasingly impatient with the Harvard *Crimson's* position that building armaments only made war inevitable. In a letter to the paper, he pointed out that Great Britain had believed the same thing and its military weakness only served to make Hitler more bold and aggressive. "Are we in America to let that lesson go unlearned?" he asked.

Jack's major project that year was his senior government thesis, on the subject of British foreign policy since 1931. His analysis basically echoed his father's belief in the inherent weakness of democracy: Dictators can marshal their countries' resources to prepare for war, the argument went, but citizens of democratic countries are intent on

Harvard Senior

During the months he spent working on his senior thesis, Jack was still forming his own opinions on war. In the end, he took a hard line against the demands of dictators: "In the light of the present day war," he wrote, "we are able to wonder at the blindness of Britain's leaders and the country as a whole that could fail to see the correctness of Churchill's arguments."

pursuing their diverse personal interests and reluctant to make the sacrifices necessary for an effective national defense. Of course there was some truth to this gloomy observation, though it had the effect of shifting the blame for unpreparedness onto a system of government and away from the failures of leaders like Neville Chamberlain and, not incidentally, Jack's own father.

Jack Kennedy was no ordinary undergraduate. Very few college seniors have the advantage of actually meeting the foreign leaders they choose to write about. With the thesis deadline looming, morever, Jack was able to rely on writing assistance from classmate Blair Clark, an editor of the *Crimson*. His roommate Torby Macdonald also pitched in, interviewing and hiring a stenographer who would translate Jack's dictation into properly spelled and, for the most part, grammatical prose. The result was a 150-page typescript, about twice as long as the usual senior thesis. Jack's professors had some reservations about his work, finding the paper "laborious" in its arguments and poorly written. Still, they were impressed by the underlying research and awarded a magna cum laude, a signal accomplishment in an era when only a small percentage of Harvard students received honors grades.

Delighted, Jack showed the thesis to his father's favorite journalist, Arthur Krock, who offered to have his agent shop around for a publisher. Informed of this development, the ambassador was enthusiastic. "You would be surprised how a book that really makes the grade with high-class people stands you in good stead for years to come," he wrote his son.

Over the next few months, Jack's thesis was transformed into a book, published under the title *Why England Slept*. The prose of the final manuscript reflected considerable polishing by Krock and others. In the process, Jack's message underwent a 180-degree shift. Instead of exposing the weakness of democracy, the book as published reflected an upbeat faith in its ability to meet the challenges posed by the rise of Nazism. In stirring prose, it urged American readers to take a lesson from Britain's mistakes and prepare for war. The words may not have been all Jack's own, but the conclusion accurately reflected his thinking. Even when he was in Europe he had much preferred Churchill to Chamberlain, and the more time he spent apart from his father, who was still serving in London, the more persuaded he became that intervention was inevitable and justified.

Why England Slept appeared in July 1940, complete with a foreword by *Time* and *Life* publisher Henry Luce, a family friend. The book quickly became a national best-seller, thanks in large part to the ambassador, who purchased tens of thousand of copies. Unopened cartons of

Why England Slept
With the publication of his thesis, Jack found himself a best-selling author at the age of 23. Some readers thought he had gone too far in exonerating his father and Chamberlain for their support of appeasement. One former professor of Jack's quipped that the book should have been called *Why Daddy Slept*.

Why England Slept would molder for years in a New York warehouse and even in the attic of Kennedys' Hyannis Port summer home. Jack, meanwhile, worked hard to promote his first book, sending out autographed copies to influential people, giving radio interviews and personally calling bookstores to make sure his work was being properly displayed.

Asked to provide a blurb for the British edition, Harold Laski delivered a brutal verdict. In a letter to Joe Kennedy, Laski bluntly told him that if it weren't for the power of nepotism, no publisher would have looked at the book. "I care a lot about your boys," Laski wrote. "I don't want them to be spoilt as rich men's sons are so easily spoilt."

However, Laski's prediction that Jack would be embarrassed by the book in years to come would be proven wrong. *Why England Slept* was by no means an original or important book, but it was a timely one. It made Jack a minor literary celebrity. In the longer run, it also positioned him firmly on the winning side of a critically important foreign policy debate.

With hindsight, the most important lesson to be drawn from Jack Kennedy's first publication was that he was willing and able to stake out a public position independent of his domineering father. In an August 1940 interview with the *Boston Globe*, Jack emphasized that he didn't share his father's opinions about "certain British statesmen." For that matter, he hadn't even seen the ambassador in six months.

Surprisingly enough, even after Ambassador Kennedy belatedly got around to reading Jack's manuscript, he remained supportive. His desire to advance his son's literary reputation trumped politics, even on an issue as important as the war. Joe's own views certainly hadn't changed. Returning to the U.S. in the fall of 1940, he aired his opinions in a lengthy conversation with three reporters, including the influential Louis Lyons of the *Boston Globe*. Joe warmed up to his subject with a few scathing remarks about Eleanor Roosevelt, describing the first lady as a foolish do-gooder. "She's always sending a note to have some little Suzie Glotz to tea at the embassy," he complained. Joe went on to predict the defeat of Britain, calling its war effort "bunk." "Democracy is finished in England. It may be here," he concluded. Such doom saying rhetoric didn't go over at all well. Although Joe later complained bitterly that he had meant his remarks to be off the record, they were duly published, effectively ending his aspirations for public office.

By the end of 1940, the accepted order of precedence within the Kennedy clan was undergoing a subtle change. Joe Kennedy, along with his eldest son and chosen heir, were identified with views that were coming to be thought of as defeatist and even unpatriotic. Meanwhile, Jack, the perennial underachiever, had enjoyed his moment of fame, portrayed by the press as a thoughtful spokesman for the youth of America.

The Ambassador

Joe Kennedy had once been considered a plausible rival to Roosevelt, who was running for an unprecedented third term. By the fall of 1940, however, he was constantly flayed in the press for being not only anti-Semitic but also anti-British. Joe publicly endorsed Roosevelt in October of that year and tendered his resignation on December 2.

Survival in the Solomons

1941–1946

A ccording to biographical accounts that appeared in the late 1950s, John F. Kennedy spent the year after his graduation from Harvard in northern California as a student at Stanford University. In reality, Jack registered as a business student in 1940 but took little interest in his courses. He had arrived in Palo Alto with a new Buick convertible, fitted out with red leather upholstery, and spent most of his time squiring attractive young women to clubs in San Francisco.

Although America was not yet in the war, a state of national emergency had been declared and many recent graduates were marking time, awaiting the summons to military service. Jack, moreover, had the usual excuse of bad health. By January 1941 he was back in Boston, hospitalized with what appeared to be stomach ulcers. Writing off the spring semester as a loss, he then decided to accompany his mother and Eunice on a tour of South America.

The draft lottery had been reinstated while Jack was in Palo Alto, and his birthday was the eighteenth to be chosen, virtually guaranteeing that he would be called up in the near future. Joe Jr., despite his isolationist views, was already in a Naval Reserve training program, preparing to become a pilot. It would be highly embarrassing if the author of *Why England Slept* failed to perform military service, but when Jack applied for Officers Candidate School he failed the Army physical. He managed to get into the

Navy only with the help of Capt. Alan Kirk, who had been a naval attaché in London and written the official report on the sinking of the *Athenia*. Kirk had a physician friend sign off on Jack's paperwork, and after a brief stint in training, Ensign John F. Kennedy was assigned to a desk job at the Office of Naval Intelligence in Washington.

Kathleen Kennedy was also in Washington, working for the *Times-Herald*, a pro-isolationist paper owned by the publishing heiress Cissy Patterson. For the first time Jack and Kick had a chance to get to know one another outside the family setting, and they soon discovered that they shared many of the same doubts and resentments. Jack was keenly aware of how the Kennedy ideal of family loyalty was often a substitute for emotional intimacy. For the moment, Kathleen's frustrations centered on the expectation that Joe and Rose's children would be role models for other Roman Catholics. Although she was leading an active social life in Washington, she could not forget that in England a duke's son wanted to marry her, and it seemed unfair that religion should stand between two people in love.

Jack empathized. While at Harvard, he'd dated Frances Ann Cannon, the beautiful, clever, and Protestant heiress to a North Carolina textile fortune. For a time, he'd even talked about wanting to marry her. Since Jack also had second- and third-string girlfriends during this period, it's hard to say how serious he was about Frances Ann. Still, if it weren't for the opposition of both families, largely on religious grounds, the romance might have ended in an engagement. Jack cared enough about Frances Ann to be jealous when she gave up on him and married a penniless writer named John Hersey.

With hindsight, it's amazing how much parental control the adult Kennedy children took for granted. Joe kept well apprised of his sons' and daughters' social lives and regularly hired private detectives to do background checks on their dates. He also discouraged them from taking an interest in business and financial affairs, on the grounds that he had taken care of the unpleasant business of making money so that his children would be free to pursue higher goals. But this reasoning also insured that the children would remain permanent dependents. They were at best dimly aware of the terms of their own trusts and had no idea how much income they were generating. Jack traveled frequently, stayed at the best hotels, and went out to restaurants and nightclubs. When the bills arrived, he simply endorsed them and sent them on to his father's office on Park Avenue in New York City. Jack, moreover, had acquired his mother's habit of

Kick & Mom
Had she lived longer, JFK's sister Kick (left, with mother Rose) might have become the first rebel in the family. Her warm, engaging personality stood in sharp contrast to the guarded exterior of her mother, and she bristled at Rose's rigid (though hardly unusual) disapproval of inter-faith marriages.

never carrying cash. Friends, including women he had invited out on dates, often found themselves paying for cab fares, meals and movie tickets. A few of Jack's pals finally realized that the only way they would ever see their money again was to submit their own bills to Joe's office. As much as Jack might chafe at the demands of being a Kennedy, a 24-year-old man who had no idea of how to manage his own expenses could afford only so much independence.

The lack of true communication within the Kennedy family was poignantly illustrated by the unfortunate fate of Rosemary. Enrolled as a student at a Sacred Heart convent in Massachusetts, the eldest Kennedy daughter appeared to be regressing mentally. Frustrated at being unable to keep up with others her age, she threw tantrums and got into the habit of slipping away from the campus to wander the neighboring streets alone in the middle of the night. Since Rosemary was a good-looking girl with a voluptuous figure, Joe and Rose naturally worried that she would be sexually molested. Kathleen, in an attempt to be helpful, suggested that her father look into a highly touted operation known as pre-frontal lobotomy that was being performed at St. Elizabeth's Hospital in Washington, D. C., by Drs. Walter J. Freeman and James W. Watts.

Lobotomy was never intended as a treatment for mental retardation; however, Dr. Watts came to the convenient but highly unlikely conclusion that Rosemary was not retarded after all but suffered from a form of depression. The surgery was performed in October 1941 with devastating results. Rosemary lost the ability to care for her personal needs and was left with limited verbal skills. Biographers have dealt harshly with Joe for authorizing his daughter's operation. Some writers have suggested that he could not tolerate having a child who was less than perfect or even that he was abusing Rosemary and wanted to silence her. But these insinuations are surely unfair. At least 40,000 patients would undergo lobotomies during the 1940s and '50s, usually at the behest of families who were desperately hoping for a miracle cure that would spare their loved one from spending life in a dreary institution. There is no reason to suppose that Joe's motivations were any different.

ROSEMARY

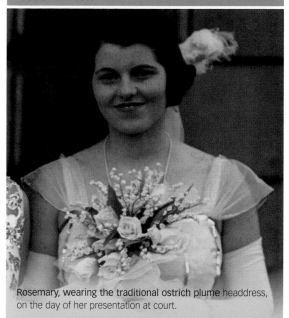

Rosemary, wearing the traditional ostrich plume headdress, on the day of her presentation at court.

Not until after John Kennedy was elected president did he or any member of his family openly acknowledge that his sister Rosemary was mentally retarded, as it was called at the time. Until that time, the Kennedys invariably described Rosemary as the shy sister who was dedicating her life to teaching disabled children at St. Coletta's School in Wisconsin. Such deception was typical of the times. In later years, however, the Kennedys have done more than their share to assure that mentally retarded children will no longer be hidden away.

Funds from the Joseph P. Kennedy, Jr., Foundation, established in 1946, were dedicated to medical research into the causes of mental retardation and promoting social awareness of the problem. Eunice Kennedy Shriver became especially active in these causes. In 1961 she urged her brother to create an advisory committee on mental retardation, and she was instrumental in getting his President's Fitness Awards program to adopt supplementary standards tailored to the needs of the developmentally disabled.

In 1968, Eunice and her husband, R. Sargent Shriver, became founders of the Special Olympics, which has grown to serve more than 1 million children around the world.

Navy Men
Like many other young men eager to serve, both Jack and Lem Billings had to resort to subterfuge to pass their physicals. At the time of this reunion, Jack had already returned from the Pacific and was nursing his bad back in Palm Beach, Florida. Lem had secretly donned contact lenses to pass the eye test and become a navy ensign.

Remarkably, however, Joe did not consult with Rose before deciding on the surgery. Nor, when it was over, leaving Rosemary unable to speak intelligibly or care for herself, could he bring himself to tell his wife what he had done. Rosemary was sent to St. Coletta's, a school for the mentally retarded in Wisconsin, where she was still living in 2002, in a private house on the school grounds. This course of events says a good deal about Joe Kennedy's controlling personality, but even more about Rose's withdrawal into a fantasy world of her own making. Although she and Eunice visited Rosemary at St. Coletta's, Rose apparently never questioned the cause of her daughter's sudden deterioration and she did not learn of the operation until many years later.

Jack would provide the occasion for the next family crisis when he became involved with Inga Arvad, a Danish journalist who had a history of association with prominent Nazis. Fluent in four languages, Arvad had introduced herself to Arthur Krock on a New York street and asked him to help her get work on a Washington newspaper. Overcome by her stunning looks, Krock recommended Arvad for a job on the *Times-Herald*, where she was assigned to write a regular feature called "Did You Happen to See…?" Her job consisted of interviewing people recently arrived in the capital to work on the war effort and writing them up in chatty, at times gushing, prose. Arvad quickly became friendly with her co-worker Kathleen Kennedy, who introduced her to Jack.

Four years older than the green Navy ensign, Inga knew how to be a temptress, a tease, a mother figure and, at times, a practitioner of emotional blackmail. Used to thinking of himself as the pursuer, Jack was caught completely off guard. He was fascinated by Inga-Binga, as he called her, and she professed in her calculatedly broken English to be "gooey with love" for him. Unfortunately, Arvad was also of interest to the FBI and the Office of Naval Intelligence. Informed of rumors about Arvad's past that were circulating at the *Times-Herald*, the FBI had put her apartment under surveillance and would eventually plant a listening device there.

Born in Copenhagen in 1913, Arvad spent her childhood traveling around Europe, attending schools in England, France, and Germany. At the age of seventeen she represented Denmark in the Miss Europe beauty pageant

and began a brief marriage to an Egyptian diplomat. By 1935 she was single again and living in Berlin with her mother, who had well-placed friends, including the chief of police. Representing herself as a correspondent for a Danish newspaper, Arvad gained an interview with Goering. She was a guest at his wedding, and got to know Himmler and Goebbels. During the 1936 Olympics, Hitler invited her to sit his private box and pronounced her an ideal Nordic beauty.

According to an interview that Arvad's son gave to Kennedy biographers Joan and Clay Blair, Jr., the German foreign minister, Joachim von Ribbentrop, tried to set Arvad up as a Nazi spy in Paris, but she refused his overtures. Instead, she married Paul Fejos, a Hungarian film director, following him to the Far East and, later, to Peru, where he was making a documentary on the lost cities of the Incas. Fejos's work in Peru attracted the attention of American intelligence agents because it was paid for by Axel Wenner-Gren, a wealthy Swede thought to be financing Nazi propaganda and espionage efforts around the world through his bank in the Bahamas. By the time Arvad met Jack Kennedy, she was separated from Fejos, though she was receiving money from Wenner-Gren, for reasons that are unclear.

It may be that Inga Arvad was an innocent whose striking beauty at the age of 22 had led to her being taken up by all the wrong people. But the FBI couldn't know this for sure, and even in retrospect, there are elements of Arvad's story that raise questions about her motives, starting with the way she seemingly homed in on Jack Kennedy, the intelligence officer son of a suspected German sympathizer. Although she was aware of the FBI's suspicions and complained that J. Edgar Hoover was persecuting her, Arvad at one point tried to talk Jack's friend Torby Macdonald into applying for a job at the bureau. On another occasion, Arvad was overheard by FBI surveillance repeating to Jack, almost word for word, a conversation about her that he'd recently had with his father. When Jack wondered how she could possibly know about this private father-son talk, Arvad teasingly told him that her estranged husband, Fejos, "has his little spies out all over the place"—hardly language to disarm the FBI's suspicions.

Inga Arvad
Inga in 1931, on winning the title of Miss Denmark. She eventually married Hollywood Western actor Tim McCoy. Her son recalled that Inga considered Jack dedicated to the betterment of humanity but cold in his personal relationships. When out in public, he would joke about having to "turn on the BP"— the Big Personality.

Guilty or innocent, Inga Arvad was not a suitable girlfriend for an intelligence specialist. But Jack was utterly infatuated, and he ignored numerous warnings, including those of his father. Then columnist Walter Winchell ran an item that described the affair without mentioning the lovers' names. The following day, January 15, 1942, Jack was transferred out of Washington and assigned to a bottom-rung job at the Sixth Naval District Headquarters in Charleston, South Carolina. Given heightened

PT Training School

In October 1942, Jack arrived at the PT-Boat Training School in Melville, Rhode Island, where he and the other students lined their mattresses with newspaper in order to get some sleep during the bitterly cold nights. Jack (7th from right, 3rd row) hoped to be assigned to the same squadron as his Harvard friend Torby Macdonald, but it was not to be.

concerns about security in the months after Pearl Harbor, he was fortunate to escape court-martial.

Even after his transfer, Jack had access to information of potential interest to the enemy. For example, while visiting his parents in Palm Beach, he had a long conversation with their houseguest, who happened to be Lord Halifax, the British ambassador. Inga, still professing her love, came down to Charleston for a visit and even hinted at marriage; however, as the FBI surveillance team had reason to know, she would be in bed with another lover within hours of her return to Washington. When Jack hesitated about making a commitment, Arvad upped the ante by leaving for Reno, Nevada, where she could obtain a speedy divorce from Paul Fejos. Jack was in turmoil. He realized that Inga's past made her "dangerous" but found it hard to imagine that a woman who was so "affectionate" and "wonderful in bed" could possibly be a spy.

The impasse ended when Jack learned of an opportunity to be trained for sea duty. The Navy was cycling desk officers through a ninety-day training program at Northwestern University in Illinois, and Jack's application was accepted in June 1942. No sooner had he left for Evanston than Inga informed him that she was marrying a Danish acquaintance, not

for love but simply because she saw the match as an opportunity to re-establish herself in New York.

At Northwestern, Jack was recruited into the PT boat service. The exploits of the PT boats had recently been celebrated in the book *They Were Expendable*, making patrol torpedo boats the assignment of choice for Ivy Leaguers who had experience with family yachts and sailboats. In actuality, the job of PT boat skipper was far from glamorous. To be aboard a plywood boat as it scudded over the waves was a bit like riding a modern jet-ski, though one that happened to be carrying live torpedoes and 3,000 gallons of flammable fuel. It was hardly a job for a man who had been periodically disabled by lower back pain even while working behind a desk. Somehow, the PT service recruiters overlooked this aspect of Jack's military records.

While his physical fitness was debatable, Jack's personality served him well once he got out of the ONI. Like his grandfather Honey Fitz, he had the ability to keep those around him happy and entertained, a great asset when it came to getting along with people from very different backgrounds. Of course, Jack's humor was more low-key than his grandfather's. His dry Ivy League sarcasm was often turned against the establishment, and he groused

No Pencil-Pusher

A helpful physician had certified Jack Kennedy for military service on the assumption that he was slated for a desk job. Even after being trained for PT-boat duty, Jack was initially assigned to duties as an instructor. Despite his medical history, Jack was determined to go overseas, and the exigencies of wartime eventually worked in his favor.

THE MOSQUITO FLEET

Patrol Torpedo boats, or PTs, were light, maneuverable vessels, sometimes known as the "mosquito fleet." Made almost entirely of plywood, the typical PT boat was 77 feet long and powered by three 1500 horsepower engines capable of accelerating from 8 to 40 knots (46 miles an hour) in approximately 11 seconds. PT boats were used in all theaters of World War II, but they achieved their greatest glory in the

The boat in the foreground is *PT-59*, which was converted into a gunboat and commanded by Jack, now Lieutenant Kennedy, after the sinking of *PT-109*.

Pacific, where they disrupted the nighttime enemy supply convoys known as the "Tokyo Express." PTs harassed destroyers 55 times their size and sometimes sank them, but they were most effective against enemy supply barges.

with the rest of the men about what they saw as the dilatory tactics of General MacArthur, whom the troops had given the derisory nickname "Dug-out Doug." Moreover, in contrast to his otherwise personable sister Kathleen, who had managed to get posted to London as a Red Cross volunteer, Jack didn't flaunt his connections or use them to obtain privileged treatment. Men who served with him had no idea that he came from an influential family until they began to wonder why he was receiving letters from Clare Boothe Luce, the wife of publisher Henry Luce, and bills from the Waldorf Astoria.

At first it seemed likely that Jack would spend the war stateside as a training officer. After eight months, however, he was shipped to Tulagi, in the Solomon Islands northeast of Guadalcanal. The day of his arrival coincided with the fiercest Japanese bombing raid in months, and his ship, heavily loaded with munitions, narrowly escaped a direct hit. Even so, one bomb

came so close that the ship lurched out of the water, and the captain was knocked off his feet and broke his neck. Shortly after this close call, the vessel attempted to pick up a Japanese flyer who had parachuted into the bay. As the ship approached, the man drew his pistol and fired at his would-be rescuers. Jack found this introduction to the enemy a sobering experience.

In April 1943, Ensign Kennedy became the commander of *PT-109*, an eighty-foot boat built by the Electric Boat Company (ELCO) in Bayonne, New Jersey. Around this time, the Navy began to push northward, forcing the Japanese back toward their main base at Rabaul. By early July, Jack's squadron was assigned to a front line outpost on the tiny island of Lumbari. The men slept in tents and ate canned rations, mostly stew and something called "corned willie." For recreation, they played endless hands of poker. Jack and a few others who didn't care for cards passed the time talking about politics and baseball.

Their assignment was to harass the nighttime convoys that carried reinforcements from Rabaul to the Japanese base at Vila on Kolombangara Island. *PT-109* had a close call in mid-July, when a Japanese plane narrowly missed hitting the craft with a pair of bombs. A stationary PT boat was difficult for nighttime air patrols to spot, but the gleaming white wake of a fast-moving boat made an easy target. After nearly being hit, Jack was especially careful to take the precautions favored by some other members of his squadron—running at low speed with just one engine in gear.

During the early-morning hours of August 3, *PT-109* was nearing the end of a largely uneventful patrol. Jack was at the wheel, running at idle speed. Apparently, some members of the crew were asleep, and the radio officer, busy conferring with the skipper, failed to take note of a message warning that a Japanese ship had been spotted in the area. Suddenly, a looming shape emerged from the darkness. It was the destroyer *Amagiri* heading straight for *PT-109* at a speed of about forty knots. Jack was unable to get his boat moving in time to take evasive action. The *Amagiri* sliced through *PT-109* and continued on its way.

Spilled fuel immediately ignited, creating a fireball that was spotted by other members of the squadron, who assumed that they had just seen the end of *PT-109* and its crew. Fortunately, however, most of the fuel was dumped near the aft section of the vessel, cut off by the *Amagiri*'s wake from the forward section of the hull, which was still afloat. Jack and the other crewmen who were left clinging to the damaged hull immediately leapt overboard, expecting a second explosion. After a few minutes in the water, realizing that what remained of *PT-109* was not going to catch fire, Jack and two others, John Maguire and Edgar Mauer, hauled themselves back onto the listing wreckage.

Jack then swam out to help Pappy McMahon, the 39-year-old engine man, who was badly injured with burns on his hands, arms and face. Jack pulled McMahon back to the hull and returned to help two more crewmen, Charles Harris and Ray Starkey. In the meantime,

G.I. Jack
In August 2000, Hasbro released this new addition to the family of G.I. action figures. The doll commemorates Jack Kennedy's exploits during the rescue of the crew of *PT-109*.

The Crew of PT-109

Jack, at far right, poses with some members of his crew. Allan Webb, in the T-shirt at far left, was the commander of another boat; he accompanied Jack on several missions. Others shown, back row, left to right, are Leon Drawdy, Edgar E. Mauer, Edmund Drewitch, and John Maguire. In front are Charles Harris, Maurice Kowal, Andrew Kirksey, and Lennie Thom.

Mauer, a non-swimmer, scanned the water with a battle lantern while Maguire, a rope tied around his waist, swam out to help others who were in danger of being swept away on the current. Within an hour, eleven men were back on board the hull. Two members of the crew, Andrew Kirksey and Harold Marney, were never seen again.

Afraid of drawing the attention of a Japanese ship, Jack decided not to fire his flare pistol. He assumed that when dawn broke, rescuers would be out looking for the missing PT boat. But by two the following afternoon, with no help in sight, he reluctantly decided that it would be folly to try to spend another night aboard the unstable hull, which looked as if it could not remain afloat for long. Since two of the sailors, Mauer and the injured William Johnston, were non-swimmers, the crew improvised a raft from two coconut tree trunks that had been used as gun mounts. Pappy McMahon was unable to cling to the raft with his burned hands, so Jack gripped the strap of McMahon's life jacket between his teeth and towed him three and a half miles to the nearest island. After about four hours in the water, the exhausted men crawled ashore on a tiny atoll, nauseated from swallowing seawater mixed with gasoline.

Unknown to Jack and his crew, an Australian coast watcher concealed on Kolombangara Island had spotted the floating remains of *PT-109* and radioed

for help. At about 6 PM, just as Jack's crew reached the atoll, an Allied air patrol was out searching for the lost PT boat. The pilot of one of the P-40 fighters, a New Zealander, spotted the hulk but saw no survivors. Nearby on the atoll, Jack and his crew had dived for cover thinking the plane belonged to the enemy. By the time they recognized the tail markings and pulled themselves out of the underbrush, it was too late.

That night, Jack took a .38 pistol and a lantern and paddled out into the Ferguson Passage, which was on the route of the nighttime PT boat patrols. It was a brave act, and probably also a foolish one since the sight of a light from an unknown source would likely have prompted the patrols to open fire without further investigation. In any event, Jack saw no one, lost his lantern, and was caught up in a swift current that nearly swept him into the Blackett Strait, headed for the coast of Japanese-occupied Kolombangara. He rode the current helplessly until, by sheer luck, the shifting tide carried him back in the direction he had come and dumped him on a reef, not far from his starting point. The next morning, Jack was able to swim back to the atoll, arriving about noon, feverish and retching.

On the third day, desperate for something to drink, the survivors took to the water again, moving to a larger island, Olasana, about a quarter of a mile away. Olasana had coconut trees, and they were able to slake their thirst by drinking the juice. On the fourth day, Jack and one of the other officers, Ensign Barney Ross, swam to a third island, Naru, where they found a metal box containing cookies and candies left behind by the fleeing Japanese, as well as a drum half full of fresh water and a broken dugout canoe. Filling the metal box with water, Jack towed it back to Olasana. When he arrived, he discovered his crew sitting around a blazing fire, happily consuming C-rations. Two islanders, scouts employed by the Australian coast watcher, had been dispatched in a dugout canoe to search for the survivors and bring them emergency supplies.

Jack later returned with the scouts to Naru. On the way, they met Barney Ross, who was in the process of swimming the quarter-mile distance back to Olasana. Before parting from the scouts, Biuki and Eroni, Jack scratched a message onto a coconut shell: NAURO [sic] ISL/ NATIVE KNOWS POSIT/ HE CAN PILOT/ 11 ALIVE/ NEED SMALL BOAT/ KENNEDY.

Biuki and Eroni carried the message back to the coast watcher. The following morning, seven islanders appeared in a large canoe, bringing more food and a cook stove. Alerted by radio, two PT boats from Lumbari were already on their way to pick up the eleven survivors.

FIRST ATOMIC FISSION

In late 1942, physicist Enrico Fermi demonstrated the first controlled nuclear chain reaction, in a makeshift lab on a squash court at the University of Chicago. The experiment paved the way for the atomic bomb.

Message on a Coconut

Jack kept the piece of coconut shell on which he had scratched a message giving his marooned crew's position; it sat on his desk in the Oval Office. In 1963 there were plans for a reunion between the president and the Pacific Islanders, Biuki and Eroni, who delivered the message. He was assassinated before the meeting could take place.

A Hero's Return

Captain F. L. Conklin awards the Navy and Marine Corps Medal to Lieutenant Kennedy at the Chelsea Naval Hospital. Friends found Jack slightly embarrassed over the glorification of his role in the PT-109 episode. Later, following the publication of Robert J. Donovan's book *PT-109*, he commented wryly that his story kept getting better.

When the story of *PT-109's* misadventure was released by the Navy, war correspondents immediately recognized a good story, and one with a celebrity hook. The Associated Press's account, written by Leif Erickson, made front-page news around the country. The *New York Times'* version carried the headline: KENNEDY'S SON IS HERO IN THE PACIFIC AS DESTROYER SPLITS HIS PT BOAT.

Jack himself commented later that the Navy couldn't decide whether to award him a medal or court-martial him. Of course, the same could probably be said of many storied episodes in military history. On the one hand, Jack had lost his boat, and it was hard for the brass to figure out how he could have let a Japanese destroyer get so close. On the other, his pluck and determination during the ordeal that followed were widely admired. Jack was indeed considered a hero on Lumbari, and he was eventually awarded the Navy and Marine Corps medal for his conduct after the fatal accident. Moreover, he had won the admiration of the true experts on the incident, his surviving crew. Five of them would follow Jack to his next command and several became lifelong friends.

Jack, on his part, came out of the ordeal a changed man. Coming so close to death had reinforced his innate skepticism about authority. Like many military personnel in the Solomons, he had long bristled when he read commentaries from stateside patriots who talked about keeping forces in the islands for ten years, if necessary, in order to root out the last of the enemy. Now, he also found it hard to forgive his fellow skippers who insisted, somewhat unconvincingly, that they had done all they could to search for his boat before returning to base on the morning of August 2. But most of all, he emerged from a few days in sick bay filled with a newfound determination to fight the Japanese. Having lost two of the men under his command, the war had become personal for him. Jack was especially sick at heart over the death of Andrew Kirksey, who was married and a father. Kirksey had been shaken up by the earlier incident when bombs fell uncomfortably near the boat, and Jack had planned to get him transferred, on the reasoning that when a sailor got the idea in his head that his luck had run out, he was all too often right.

Although he was eligible for leave, Jack stayed in the Solomons and was given command of a PT that had been refitted as a gunboat, its torpedoes removed and extra armament added on deck. As skipper of *Gunboat No. 1*, he saw action during the evacuation of Marines from Choiseul. By December,

however, his deteriorating physical condition could no longer be ignored. He was wearing a brace to support his troublesome lower back and needed a cane to hobble around the base. Also, in addition to the usual stomach pains, indications of a suspected duodenal ulcer, he was troubled by spastic colitis, whose symptoms included debilitating abdominal cramps. PT boat activity in the Solomons was winding down and the unit's commander added Jack's name to a list of men whose services were no longer needed. He left the islands two days before Christmas, reaching San Francisco on January 7, 1944.

On his way to see his parents in Palm Beach, Jack paid a call to Inga Arvad, now a Los Angeles-based gossip columnist whose work appeared as backup for the popular Sheila Graham. Arvad was still single, never having carried out her threat to marry her Danish boyfriend. But Jack was not the same starry-eyed lover who had risked his career for his "Inga-Binga." Arvad prattled on about her belief that she and Jack had been unfairly persecuted by J. Edgar Hoover and the FBI. But such complaints seemed rather irrelevant from the point of view of man who was faced with writing letters and making calls to the families and girlfriends of seamen who had been left behind in the Solomons.

By February Jack—now promoted to lieutenant—was in New York, where he had dinner with the former Frances Ann Cannon and her husband. John Hersey was fascinated by Jack's experiences, especially his description of his nighttime swim in the Ferguson Passage. Hersey saw the swim as a metaphor: Men struggle to survive, but fate is inexorable and fickle. No one knows why some are rescued while others are swept away.

Hersey wrote a powerful account of the incident, telling as much of the story as military censors would permit. Entitled "Survival," the article appeared in the *New Yorker* and succeeded in establishing the ordeal of the *PT-109* crew as one of the more memorable episodes of the South Pacific campaign. Jack gave his approval to the text, though he was a little embarrassed by it, feeling that Hersey had concentrated too much on him to the exclusion of others like Ensign Lennie Thom, who had kept the group together while he was off reconnoitering.

Joe Kennedy had no such feelings of humility. Without consulting Hersey, his agent, or the *New Yorker*, Joe took it upon himself to persuade the *Reader's Digest* that it ought to print a condensed version. The deal was consummated only after delicate

John Hersey

During the summer of 1939, Jack learned that his girlfriend Frances Ann Cannon was throwing him over to marry John Hersey, a penniless writer five years her senior. Jack attended the wedding and remained friendly with Hersey, who went on to enjoy a prestigious career, winning the Pulitzer Prize for his first novel, *A Bell for Adano*. Hersey's marriage to Frances Ann ended in divorce in 1956. He published 26 books before his death in 1993.

negotiations between the *Digest* and the *New Yorker*, whose editors disapproved of the very idea of condensations. Hersey, who can only have been astounded by the ambassador's gall, generously agreed to donate proceeds from the reprint to the widow of Andrew Kirksey.

After his 30-day leave ended, Jack was theoretically assigned to the PT operations base in Melville, Rhode Island. In fact, he spent most of his time in and out of hospitals. During one of these hospital stays, Dr. James Poppen of Boston's exclusive Lahey Clinic did extensive tests and concluded that Jack's back pain was caused by tissue from a ruptured disc that was irritating a nerve.

While Jack debated whether to have surgery, the family was in an uproar. Kathleen Kennedy, who was serving as a Red Cross volunteer in London, had announced that she was planning to marry her aristocratic sweetheart, Billy Hartington. The Red Cross had strict rules designed to prevent female volunteers from using their assignments to reunite with their husbands and boyfriends, but Kathleen had managed to work her away around these restrictions, rekindling the interrupted romance. Billy's unit, the Coldstream Guards, was slated to take part in the imminent invasion of the Continent, and he and Kathleen decided to marry beforehand. The registry office ceremony took place on May 6, 1944, a month before D-Day.

Joe Kennedy accepted the inevitable; perhaps he was even secretly proud of his favorite daughter's enterprise in snaring a duke's son. Honey Fitz was also prepared to be open-minded. He gave a rambling interview to the press, reaching the conclusion that Kathleen was a good Catholic and a "quality" girl, and therefore, presumably, any young man she chose also represented "quality," despite his religion. Rose, however, saw the marriage as a tragedy and took refuge from the press by checking into New England Baptist Hospital. In fairness to Rose, interfaith marriage was still very much a live issue, and as a prominent Catholic laywoman she was the family member who not only had to field reporters' questions but also the condolences of friends and churchmen who were doubtless too polite to say outright that she had failed in her duty as a mother. Still, Kathleen began her

Wartime Wedding

On May 6, 1944, Kathleen, who had returned to London as a Red Cross volunteer, married her aristocratic fiancé, Billy Hartington, in a ten-minute registry office ceremony. Rose was inconsolable when she learned that her daughter had married a Protestant.

married life puzzling over press reports, some of which implied that the news of the wedding had made Rose ill. The newlyweds surely had enough on their minds without this added worry.

Rose was out of the hospital but still recovering from the shock of Kathleen's marriage to a Protestant when Jack checked into New England Baptist. His surgery, performed on June 23, appeared to be successful at first, but within a few weeks he was once again bedridden with back pain and spasms of the lower abdominal tract. The surgical incision on his back stubbornly refused to heal, and Jack's high fevers as well as the yellowish-tan color of his skin prompted the doctors to conclude that he was having a recurrence of malaria, even though there is no record that he had suffered from the disease in the South Pacific. After almost two months confined to a hospital bed, the patient was weak but also thoroughly bored and restless, and his doctors gave him permission to check out of the hospital for a restful weekend visit with his family on Cape Cod.

And so it happened that Jack was at the Kennedy home in Hyannis Port on the 13th of August when a pair of Navy chaplains arrived, bearing the news that Joe Jr.'s plane had exploded in midair while on a secret mission aimed at knocking out a German rocket-launching site. Joe Kennedy spoke with the chaplains, then broke the news to his children, who had gathered on the Cape to take part in a sailboat race that afternoon. Joe urged the children to go ahead and compete, on the theory that Joe would want them to be brave and soldier on with their plans.

But for once, Joe couldn't follow his own advice. Devastated, he retreated to his bedroom to mourn. Two weeks later, some of Jack's buddies from the PT boat service came for a weekend visit, and Joe exploded with rage when he heard them singing out on the lawn. His eldest son, the child who had been slated to become president of the United States, was gone, and it was intolerable that anyone should ever be happy and carefree again. For years to come, Joe would rail bitterly against Roosevelt, denouncing him as "the son of a bitch who killed my son Joe."

Privately, and for slightly different reasons, both Joe and Jack had cause to wonder if they were indirectly responsible for Joe Jr.'s death. Plenty of young men volunteered for suicidal missions as a matter of patriotic duty, but Joe Jr.

Joe and Roosevelt
President Roosevelt congratulates Joseph P. Kennedy, who has just been sworn in as ambassador to Great Britain by Stanley Reed, Justice of the Supreme Court, center. Joe Kennedy's appointment stunned FDR's supporters, but it was in line with the president's habit of neutralizing his critics by drafting them into positions of responsibility.

JOE JR.'S LAST MISSION

Joe Jr. in 1942, in training to be a Navy pilot.

During the summer of 1944 London was terrified by "buzz bomb" attacks. Germany's V-1 rockets were primitive guided missiles, launched from steam-powered carriages that resembled ski lifts when viewed from the air. Although the V-1s were not very efficient, rumors flew that the Germans were rushing more advanced models into production, capable of traveling at supersonic speeds.

Joseph Kennedy Jr. had been flying Navy Liberators, searching for U-boats in the Bay of Biscay, and much to his frustration, the war so far had been largely uneventful for him. About to be transferred home after completing 35 missions, he volunteered for a secret flight aimed at destroying a V-series launching site in France. A Liberator aircraft, code-named "Zoot-Suit

Black," had been fitted out as a flying bomb. The job of Joe and his co-pilot, Wilford J. Willy, was to fly their cargo of dynamite out over the English Channel. There they were supposed to bail out, so that escort planes could guide the Liberator to its target by remote control.

Joe knew that his plane's electrical system was a jerry-built affair, but he was willing to take the gamble. Unfortunately, he lost. Zoot-Suit Black blew up over the coast of England in an explosion so massive that no trace of Joe or his co-pilot's remains was ever found. Three weeks later, Allied forces captured the rocket-launching site and discovered that it had been abandoned before Joe took off.

also had personal motives. He had spent the war years stationed in England, where the Kennedy name was still associated with cowardice and appeasement, a stain he hoped to erase. Despite flying numerous missions, young Joe had seen no significant combat, and in the final days of his term of active duty, he was painfully aware of the fact that his sickly, perennially irreverent younger brother was being hailed in the States as a war hero while he had accomplished nothing of note.

Kick, the last family member to speak with Joe, arranged through the Red Cross to fly back to the U.S. in order to console her grieving parents and siblings. She was in New York, looking for silk stockings to take back to England as gifts, when a telegram arrived informing her that Captain William Cavendish, Lord Hartington, had been shot and killed by a German sniper. Her fairytale marriage was over. Billy's younger brother would inherit his properties as well as his title, so there was no practical reason for Kathleen to continue to live in England. Nevertheless, she would remain there after returning for her husband's funeral. Kick loved her family but found it impossible to live close to them. There were too many issues that could never be openly discussed, and too much pressure to live up to the public image that the family chose to project to the world.

Meanwhile, shortly after his brother's death, Jack had been forced to return to the hospital for an operation on his rectum, an undignified ordeal and hardly worth complaining about in comparison with the grief his parents and siblings were enduring. Jack quipped about being a physical "wreck," just so much raw material for a team of surgeons a little too eager to cut, and from his hospital bed he set out to pay tribute to his brother by putting together a privately published volume of reminiscences.

Although Jack spent hundreds of hours and $5,000 in an effort to create a permanent literary memorial to Joe, the effort won him little respect from his parents. The books weren't ready for Christmas, and even though Jack had been ill most of the year, Rose chided him for his thoughtlessness in failing to buy presents for the family, comparing him unfavorably with Red Fay, a buddy from the PT service who had shown up with an array of gift-wrapped trinkets. When the memorial volume was finally ready, it isn't clear that Joe ever read it. The memories it evoked were too painful. The only way to restore some of Joe's old zest for life was for Jack to step into his older brother's shoes.

Jack and Joe Jr.
While visiting their parents in Palm Beach in December 1942, the eldest Kennedy brothers posed together in their navy uniforms. It would be the last time they saw each other.

SENATOR
JOHN
F. KENNEDY

Drafted into Politics

1945–1953

A few weeks after Joe Jr.'s death, his father summoned Jack and informed him that it was his responsibility to fulfill the destiny that had been laid out for young Joe. He was to become the first Catholic president of the United States. During the 1950s, both father and son spoke freely about this fateful interview, with Jack describing how he reluctantly abandoned his vague plans to become a journalist. "It was like being drafted," he told reporter Bob Considine. "My father wanted his eldest son in politics. 'Wanted' isn't the right word. He demanded it."

Jack had always been more ambitious and competitive than he cared to admit. It may even have been true, as Red Fay later maintained, that Jack would have eventually gone into politics even had Joe Jr. lived. But it was one thing to try for political office as the second son, and a different order of pressure entirely to become the family standard bearer. Jack still harbored ambivalent feelings about his domineering father. And Joe, in turn, was less than understanding about his son's poor health. Around this time he taunted one of Jack's girlfriends, asking her "Why don't you get yourself a live one?"

By the end of 1944, the Navy had given up on Lt. Kennedy's chances for making a full recovery, and he was formally separated from the service. A civilian again, Jack departed for the Castle Hot Springs Hotel in Arizona. One of his doctors had recommended

United Nations
In celebration of the founding conference of the United Nations, the flags of the participating countries were flown in front of San Francisco's City Hall. Jack was covering the event as a special correspondent for the Hearst newspaper chain.

that he spend a year in the bracing, allergen-free climate of the Southwest, recuperating and avoiding stressful activities. Nevertheless, soon after he arrived in Arizona, Jack was perusing packets of information about Massachusetts' Eleventh Congressional District, forwarded to him by Honey Fitz's secretary. He also made fitful stabs at writing. An article he wrote opposing postwar rearmament made the rounds of *Life*, the *Readers Digest* and the *Atlantic Monthly*, receiving a tepid response despite Jack's famous name and high-level connections. Not only was the writing pedestrian, but the piece also took a position that Jack himself would soon repudiate.

Any lingering attraction Jack may have felt toward a career in journalism was dispelled in May, when he snagged an assignment to cover the founding of the United Nations in San Francisco as a special correspondent for the Hearst newspapers. Even though Jack had already met many of the American and British delegates to the conference, he soon realized that his status as a reporter didn't count for much. By day, he was reduced to trolling for the same tidbits of leaked information that U.S. delegation member Adlai Stevenson was doling out to the entire press corps. At an evening dinner party, moreover, he watched helplessly as Averell Harriman, the U.S. ambassador to Moscow, moved in on his date, escorting her out onto the balcony for a private moment. The experience dispelled any illusions Jack may have had about the glamour of a journalistic career.

By September 1945, Jack was back in Boston, testing the waters for a run for Congress in the November 1946 elections. The first difficulty he faced was that he hadn't actually lived in the Boston area since he was ten years old. He didn't know the city and had never resided in the Eleventh District, a largely working-class area that included heavily Irish Charlestown as well as Italian neighborhoods in the North End, Boston's Chinatown, parts of Somerville and a few precincts in Cambridge. Jack established legal residency by taking a two-room suite in the Bellevue Hotel, which also happened to be the home of his grandfather Honey Fitz.

Since they had sold their Bronxville, New York, house in the early 1940s, the Kennedys' primary residence had been in Palm Beach, Florida, where it was possible to take advantage of more favorable tax rates. But Joe Kennedy had always been careful to downplay the amount of time his family spent in Florida. He and Rose did little entertaining in their house on North Ocean

Drive, and they spent even less on decorating. Twenty years away from Boston had not prevented Joe from thinking of the city as his home territory, and he had continued to dabble in local politics, usually working through agents like his cousin Joe Kane, who was on the staff of Democratic congressman Peter Tague. In the fall of 1945, Joe's main goal was to pave the way for Jack by easing out the Eleventh District incumbent, who was none other than Honey Fitz's old nemesis James Michael Curley. Curley was facing federal mail fraud charges, which would make it difficult for him to continue to serve in Congress. Joe's solution was to encourage Curley to run for a fourth term as mayor. Bostonians did not hold Curley's legal troubles against him, and he was duly elected.

Jack, meanwhile, was busy assembling a staff. Honey Fitz and Joe Kane recommended some experienced local operatives like Billy Sutton and Patsy Mulkern, men with an intimate knowledge of Eleventh District neighborhoods. Another aide, Ken O'Donnell, had attended Harvard with Jack's brother Bobby. Red Fay and several other veterans who knew Jack from the PT boat corps also went to work for him. At this stage of his career, Jack lacked polish. He delivered his speeches in a rapid-fire monotone and was ill at ease with working-class voters. Still, he worked hard, and his disarming wit went far to win over skeptics. Jack never tried to pretend that he was anything other than a child of privilege. At one rally, after listening to a round of introductions heavy on sentimental tributes to various speakers' roots in the mean streets of Charlestown, Jack broke the ice by observing affably, "I seem to be the only person here who didn't come up the hard way."

With ten candidates vying for the safe Democratic seat, Joe Kennedy's money would be the obvious deciding factor in the campaign. Indeed, Joe later boasted that he spent so much on the 1946 race that he could have gotten his chauffeur elected. Honey Fitz also did his part by tirelessly canvassing older voters, including longtime Democratic precinct workers. Jack's younger aides tended to think of Fitz as an embarrassing link to the corruption of the past, but the Kennedy camp didn't mind resorting to old-fashioned machine tactics on occasion. The prospects of one of Jack's opponents, a city councilman named Joe Russo, were sharply diminished when Kennedy's people recruited another Joe Russo to file for the race, confusing the voters and fatally dividing the pro-Russo vote.

While Joe stayed out of the public eye, Rose Kennedy was ubiquitous. In private life, Rose was a scatterbrain who wrote notes to herself and walked around with them safety-pinned to her clothing.

Boss Curley
Before Jack could launch his career in politics, he had to finesse his way around James Michael Curley, the legendary Democratic boss whose career inspired Edwin O'Connor's novel *The Last Hurrah*. The man responsible for humiliating Honey Fitz in the "Toodles affair" was still very much in power and occupying the congressional seat that Joe Sr. wanted for his son. Joe quietly supported Curley's successful campaign for mayor of Boston.

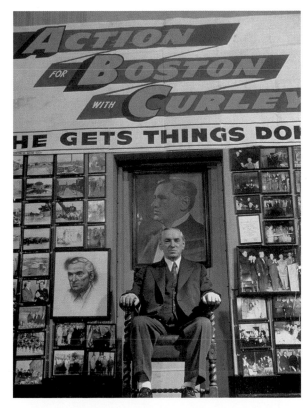

She wore the little anti-wrinkle patches known as "frownies" pasted to her face all day long, and went out in public with her hair in curlers. When the occasion demanded it, however, Rose would appear meticulously dressed in designer outfits and piquant, attention-getting hats, displaying all the political skills she had learned in the days when she served as her father's hostess and unofficial aide. Jack's campaign mailed out invitations to women voters, asking them to come have tea with Mrs. Kennedy. These "teas" filled hotel ballrooms, but Rose handled herself with the aplomb of a dowager queen, shaking hands with hundreds of women who lined up to meet her.

Wherever Rose appeared, her speeches were light on politics and heavy on domestic anecdotes. She gave housekeeping tips that were often ludicrously inappropriate to her audience, such as advice on how to pack for a summer-long tour of Europe. But when Rose talked about how she lectured her daughters that it wasn't necessary to smoke and drink to be sophisticated, one can be sure that many of her listeners nodded in agreement and duly reported her views to their own girls at home.

Money and family connections helped Jack enormously, but neither of these advantages could generate charisma, a quality he had in abundance despite his lack of experience in greeting voters. Of course, it also helped that he was a war hero in an election year when returning veterans were just beginning to make their mark in politics. More than a year had passed since Jack returned to the States, and his skinny frame and yellowish-brown complexion were primarily attributable to his mysterious blood disorder. In the minds of the public, however, an emaciated, slightly jaundiced appearance was the inevitable mark of a veteran recently returned from the Pacific theater, where soldiers were given an anti-malarial medication that turned their skins yellow. Since Jack had been busy fighting for his country in the Solomon Islands, Eleventh District voters were rightly unimpressed by his opponents' charges that he lacked experience. Even the revelation that Jack had a black valet, George Taylor, who had worked for him since his days as a Harvard undergraduate, could not outweigh his military record.

On primary day Jack captured forty percent of the vote, a considerable accomplishment for a newcomer in a ten-candidate field. After this victory, the general election was almost a formality. He carried the heavily Democratic district by almost three to one over his Republican opponent, Lester W. Bowen.

When the 80th Congress began its work in January 1947, 29-year-old John Fitzgerald Kennedy was finally ready to embark on his first full-time civilian job. Some wondered if he was mature enough to handle it. Kennedy shocked older representatives by showing up in the congressional dining room dressed in sneakers

Running for Congress
Rose, Jack, and Joe talk up Jack's candidacy. Jack's religion was an asset in his heavily Catholic district, but this would not always be the case. Some prominent Catholics opposed his presidential ambitions, fearful that by running he would inspire an anti-Catholic backlash.

GREEN CROSS
DRUGS
ICE CREAM
CANDY

A Practiced Campaigner
By the time he ran for the Senate, Jack had become much more skilled at making small talk with voters. Here he is seen campaigning in a New Bedford neighborhood in October 1952.

and a raggedy sweater. Along with two other youthful-looking first-termers, he was often mistaken for a page. To avoid such embarrassing mistakes in the future, Congress soon decreed that pages would henceforth wear a uniform consisting of a blue serge jacket with black tie.

Even Rep. Kennedy's office manager, a young woman named Mary Davis, found his attitude "rather lackadaisical." Although she was about the same age as her new boss, Davis was already a veteran Capitol Hill staffer, having previously worked for three other congressmen. She soon realized that this job was going to be her most challenging. Jack preferred talking football to obsessing about the details of pending legislation, and he was often visibly bored during meetings. He and Billy Sutton, who had joined his congressional staff, also shared a passion for practical jokes. Sutton did a wicked imitation of Vito Marcantonio, the Marxist congressman from the Bronx, and Jack would put him up to phoning colleagues like Rep. George Smathers of Florida, pretending to be Marcantonio with some bizarre request.

Jack was quite happy to let Davis handle many matters that a congressman would normally deal with personally. In addition, she often found herself playing den mother. Jack rarely remembered to carry cash, and he was often forced to borrow money to pay for his lunch dates. Davis also spent a good deal of time making calls in order to locate various items of lost property. "He was constantly replacing or trying to retrieve his coats," Davis later told Kennedy biographers Joan and Clay Blair, Jr. "He'd leave them, or his camera or a radio, on a plane or on a pushcart someplace. He very rarely carried a briefcase in those days. Thank God! That would have been lost, too."

Nevertheless, when it came time to write his first speech, Kennedy called Davis into his office and began to dictate in fluent, complete sentences. His ideas were well organized and elegantly expressed. Davis was completely taken by surprise. She thought, "*This, coming from you?*" Her opinion of her boss began to change at that moment. Despite his air of disengagement, he was "brilliant."

Jack had been elected as a moderately conservative Democrat. In keeping with sentiments in his district, he favored the expansion of Social Security benefits, public housing, and increases in the minimum wage. But he could never muster much enthusiasm for social welfare programs, and his real passion was foreign affairs. Once the outline of the Soviet Union's post war policies became clear, he emerged as a resolute cold warrior. He favored a strong national defense and vigorous opposition to communism, both abroad and at home.

Jack's most important first-term committee assignment was a seat on the House Labor and Education Committee. The other newcomer on the committee was a first-term Republican from California named Richard Nixon. Kennedy and Nixon made an odd couple. In his 1978 memoir, entitled *RN*, Nixon would refer to himself and Jack as "a pair of unmatched bookends." The rookie congressmen differed on many issues, including legislation aimed at restricting the right to strike, which Jack opposed. For the most part, however, they got along rather well thanks to their shared passion for rooting out communist infiltrators in the labor movement. Jack's sharp questioning of witnesses who testified before the committee on this subject marked the most high-profile moments of his first year in office, especially when he scored points against one of his former Harvard professors, tripping him up with a blind quotation from Lenin.

In September 1947, Jack and two of his House colleagues planned a fact-finding tour of Europe, dedicated to investigating communist influence on the labor movement. Before joining his traveling companions, Jack stopped off in Ireland, where his sister Kathleen was spending the summer with friends at Lismore, the Duke of Devonshire's romantic 11th-century castle in County Waterford. Kathleen had completed her transformation into a British socialite who unself-consciously uttered exclamations like "Oh, ducks!" Moreover, as Jack now learned, she had fallen in love with another nobleman, Peter Milton, Lord Fitzwilliam. Dashing and reputed to be

A Rising Rival

In 1952, John F. Kennedy was elected to the Senate, but voters that year also liked Ike (left), and his running mate, Richard M. Nixon of California. Nixon had started his career in Congress the same year as Jack, and the two were inevitably seen as rivals. In truth, they got along reasonably well and often appealed to the same segment of the public.

fabulously wealthy, Fitzwilliam, as he was called in England, had been a commando during World War II and loved racing fast automobiles. He was also in the process of shedding an alcoholic wife. Even though Jack foresaw another family upheaval, he was supportive of Kathleen's determination to marry her lover as soon as his divorce came through.

One day, while Kathleen and her guests were out golfing, Jack set out in hopes of discovering some of his Irish relatives in the vicinity of New Ross, about fifty miles away. His companion for the day was Pamela Churchill, the divorced wife of Winston Churchill's son. Pamela would later marry none other than Averell Harriman, the man who had stolen the attention of Jack's date in San Francisco, and enjoy a long career as Washington power hostess and Democratic fundraiser. At the time, however, she was not overly impressed with Jack Kennedy. Like many of Kathleen's friends, she assumed that Jack was Kick's younger brother. His status as a U.S. congressman did not quite register. Following directions provided by his Aunt Loretta, Jack negotiated the narrow country lanes and eventually located a family named Kennedy living in a thatched roof cottage without indoor plumbing. It wasn't entirely clear that these particular Kennedys were related to his ancestor, Patrick Joseph. Still, Jack was touched by their warmth and hospitality. Not so Pamela, who commented as they were driving away that the scene was "just like *Tobacco Road*."

Soon after this expedition, Jack became so ill that he flew to London, where Pamela gave him a recommendation to her personal physician, Sir Daniel Davis. After examining the patient, Davis delivered a brutal verdict: He was suffering from Addison's disease. The eminent doctor confided to Churchill that her friend was gravely ill, and would not last out the year. Transferred to the hospital ward of the *Queen Mary*, Jack was so ill that when the ship docked in New York, a priest came on board to administer last rites.

As far as is known, this was the first time Jack had been told that he had Addison's, a diagnosis that explained a great many mysteries in his extensive medical history. Fortunately, the physicians Jack consulted in the States were more optimistic than Dr. Davis. New treatments were just then coming onto the market. Jack was prescribed a medication called DOCA (desoxycorticosterone acetate), which came in the form of pellets that had to be injected into the muscle tissue of his thigh. Daily doses of oral cortisone would soon be added to the regimen. Even so, Jack was led to believe that he would die young, most likely in his mid-forties.

Continuing health problems sapped Jack's energy and made it difficult for him to devote

COLD WAR WOES

The autumn of 1949 brought new fears of Communist aggression, with the determination in September that the Soviet Union had detonated an atomic bomb, followed a week later by the fall of China's Nationalist government to the Communist forces of Mao Tse-tung.

Pamela Churchill

Pamela Digby Churchill, with her son, Winston Churchill II, in 1948. When Jack Kennedy met Pamela, in 1947, she had recently been divorced from Randolph Churchill, son of the former prime minister. The beautiful redhead was a contemporary of Kathleen Kennedy and several years younger than Jack. But, as she later explained, the women in her circle were interested in older men, and she had thought of Jack as a boy— "Kathleen's kid brother."

himself full-time to his congressional duties. Still, he managed well enough with the assistance of a supplemental staff, paid for by his father, who worked out of Joe's office on Park Avenue in New York City. This group was headed by James Landis, a veteran New Dealer originally hired to ghostwrite Joe Kennedy's memoirs. The arrangement was quite legal, though if it had become widely publicized it probably would have raised suspicions that Jack was acting as his father's puppet. In fact, Jack was not afraid to disagree with his father on policy matters. What set him apart from other congressmen was that he had planned to run for president from the day he made his first political speech; therefore, it was vitally important that he avoid taking positions that would hurt him later on when he became a candidate for national office. Landis's group researched the issues, occasionally consulting Harvard professors and other outside experts, and helped Jack craft middle-of-the-road positions. For example, Jack opposed direct funding of parochial schools, while mollifying his Catholic constituents by favoring subsidies for support services like school lunches and bus transportation.

One day in May 1948, Jack was at home listening to the soundtrack of the musical *Brigadoon* when he learned that a private plane carrying Kick and her lover had crashed in France, killing them both. An English friend of Kathleen's, hoping to protect her memory from scandal, explained to an inquiring reporter that Kathleen had been planning to visit her father, who was in Paris on business, when Lord Fitzwilliam, a casual friend, offered her a seat on his plane. The Kennedys adopted this fiction and held to it for years. The last man Kathleen had loved was simply written out of their version of her life.

While Kathleen's affair was a private matter, Jack's health was of legitimate interest to the voters of his district. The young congressman's gaunt appearance was the subject of intense gossip in Washington, but his office, when forced to comment at all, dismissed his periodic illnesses as recurrences of the malaria that he had allegedly contracted during the war. Similarly, Jack's troublesome back was now blamed on the mishap that had ended his career as a junior varsity football player at Harvard. Jack worked on his tan whenever possible, hoping to disguise the telltale skin tone that was a marker for Addison's.

In 1948 and again in 1950, Jack won reelection to the House. In 1952 he successfully ran for the

Sisterly Support
Jack's sisters—Patricia, Eunice and Jean left to right—sporting skirts appliquéd with his autograph. The large, energetic Kennedy family functioned almost as a shadow campaign organization. His sisters were especially effective in mobilizing women voters, holding numerous receptions and fund-raisers.

KATHLEEN KENNEDY

After her husband's death in combat, Kathleen, now known as the Marchioness of Hartington, devoted herself to Red Cross work for the remainder of the war. Even when performing serious volunteer work, Kick was always the center of attention.

On May 13, 1948, Kathleen "Kick" Kennedy and her lover, Lord Fitzwilliam, departed from England on a chartered twin-engine DeHavilland Dove for a long-planned weekend in Cannes. The plane had been slightly damaged in a thunderstorm not long before, and its pilot, Peter Townshend, was nervous about weather reports that predicted heavy squalls over the Rhone Valley. Eager to get to Cannes before the storms broke in late afternoon, Townshend planned a brief stop at Le Bourget airport near Paris, but Kick and Fitzwilliam impulsively drove into the city for a three-and-a-half-hour lunch at the Café de Paris. By the time they returned all commercial flights had been canceled, but the couple, in high spirits and looking forward to their vacation on the Riviera, badgered the reluctant pilot into taking off. Trouble began when the radio operator, Arthur Freeman, lost contact with the ground and the plane flew into a cloudbank before Townshend could adjust his altitude. Disoriented and flying blind, he unintentionally sent the plane into a steep dive, crashing into a mountainside. All four on board were killed.

"THAT'S MY BROTHER"

Bobby Kennedy put his career on hold to serve as his brother's campaign manager.

Even though Jack had been voted the most admired U.S. senator in a Roper public opinion poll, many voters were still more familiar with his brother Bobby. Robert Kennedy had been in the media spotlight in his roles as general counsel to Sen. Joe McCarthy and, later, chief counsel during the McClellan committee's probe into labor racketeering.

The confusion was decidedly a mixed blessing since Bobby's activities were unpopular with some key Democratic constituencies. Jack himself told the story of one enthusiastic voter who was determined to give him credit for Bobby's career. "I admired your work for Joe McCarthy," the voter said, pumping his hand. "No," said Jack nervously, "That's my brother." "Well then, I liked the way you went after Jimmy Hoffa and those crooks in the Teamsters' Union." "No, said Jack, "*That* was my brother, too." "I see," the voter replied. "Well tell your brother I'll be voting for him in the primary." "Oh no!" Jack corrected him. "That's me."

Senate, defeating the incumbent Henry Cabot Lodge, Jr., a liberal Republican and scion of one of Boston's most prominent Yankee families. As in 1946, family members pitched in to help get out the vote. The Kennedy sisters joined Rose in courting the female vote with a series of teas. Sargent Shriver, soon to marry Eunice Kennedy, was a speechwriter. Young Teddy worked in the office. Jack, however, was making an effort to put some distance between his father and the day-to-day operations of the campaign. After Joe lost his temper with Mark Dalton, a key member of the campaign staff, Jack asked his brother Bobby, then a lawyer working for the Department of Justice, to take over as his campaign manager. No one was more of a Kennedy loyalist than the 26-year-old Bobby, but he also did not shy away from confrontations, even with his father.

With Bobby acting as a buffer, Jack and his staff felt psychologically liberated. Even so, Joe continued to operate behind the scenes. Immediately after the *Boston Post* switched its endorsement from Lodge to Kennedy, Joe loaned half a million dollars to the paper's financially strapped owner, John Fox. When the existence of the loan was revealed in 1958, Fox insisted that it had nothing to do with his change of heart, an assertion that many observers found hard to believe.

Jack Kennedy was now 35 years old. Most of his contemporaries had married after the war, but Jack's relationships with women had become more superficial and his compulsive womanizing could no longer be dismissed as the youthful sowing of wild oats. He bedded nurses who cared for him during his hospital stays, at least one secretary in his campaign office, starlets, fashion models, the occasional high-priced prostitute and any number of actresses, among them the ice skater Sonja Henie. Many of these encounters were devoid of romance or even sensuality. Jack had spent most of his life at war with his own body, and apart from the sexual act, he did not like to be touched.

When it came to forming emotional ties, he was a bundle of insecurities. Jack worried that poor women were after his money, while rich ones might be too demanding. His preference for actresses and other career women was based on the assumption that they were less likely to be marriage-minded. Of course, the

women didn't always cooperate. In 1946, for example, Jack dated the exquisitely beautiful but emotionally fragile movie star Gene Tierney. Gene visited Hyannis Port, met Joe, and came to believe that Jack was seriously considering marrying her, even though she was in the process of divorcing designer Oleg Cassini. Jack, of course, had nothing of the sort in mind. In fact, Cassini happened to be an old friend of Joe's, and often lined up dates for him.

One can think of many psychological explanations for Jack's incessant pursuit of women. It is even possible that after 1948 the steroidal medications he took for his Addison's disease caused a hormonal imbalance that increased his sex drive and impeded his judgment. But the most obvious reason for his behavior was that he was simply replicating what he had seen at home. Jack was often embarrassed by his father. When he brought girlfriends to Hyannis Port, he found it necessary to warn them to lock their bedroom doors because the old man had a habit of prowling in the middle of the night and trying to crawl into bed with attractive female visitors. But no matter how outrageous Joe's antics became, he never suffered any serious consequences. Friends, some of them quite prominent, helpfully provided Joe Kennedy with the phone numbers of the attractive young women he wined and dined during his frequent stays in New York. Even Jack and Bobby lined up dates for their dad.

In the presence of their startled wives, Jack would invite his male friends out to parties or nightclubs. Since he was never without female companionship for long, it was implicit that such evenings out would involve the pursuit of women. Yet it didn't seem to occur to Jack that he was being rude or putting his friends in an awkward position. His assumption seemed to be that sexual conquest was a sport, like golf, that all men indulged in from time to time. It is little wonder that Jack, despite his good looks and abundant charm, had trouble sustaining close relationships with women.

Still, a man who wanted to run for president needed a wife, and Jack was approaching the stage of his career when his bachelor status would become a liability. Among those eager to play matchmaker were Charlie Bartlett, who had met Jack in Palm Beach after the war, and his wife Martha. During the summer of 1951, the Bartletts invited Jack to an intimate dinner party in their Georgetown home, using the opportunity to introduce him to Jacqueline Bouvier. Jackie—a nickname she disliked but could not shake—was just a few weeks shy of her 22nd birthday and finishing up her senior year at George Washington

University. Nothing much came of this first meeting; most accounts trace the beginning of a romantic attachment to a second dinner party that the Bartletts threw in May 1952.

By this time, ironically, Jackie was working for the *Washington Times-Herald*, where she had her own features column similar to the one Inga Arvad had written a decade earlier. Wielding a professional Speed-Graphic camera, Jackie interviewed everyone from tourists to members of Congress, soliciting responses to her provocative question of the day. With hindsight, some of these questions seem prescient, though perhaps because they drew on universal fantasies. "Which First Lady would you most like to have been?" she asked one day. And another, "If you had a date with Marilyn Monroe, what would you talk about?" Jackie spoke about becoming a writer, and at times she showed remarkable enterprise. Unaware of the taboo against women reporters entering professional baseball teams' locker rooms, she marched into the inner sanctum of the Washington Senators and got ten team members to contribute quotes for her column. Even so, her co-workers found it difficult to take her ambitions seriously. Self-contained and rather enigmatic, she had a remarkable knack for meeting famous people, especially older men. Journalistic colleagues assumed that her real mission was finding a husband.

Superficially, Jack and Jackie came from very different backgrounds. The Kennedys were new money; Jackie Bouvier was in the Social Register. In reality, however, they had a lot in common. James T. Lee, Jackie's maternal grandfather, was an Irish-American who worked his way through City College in New York before making a fortune in banking and real estate. The aristocratic heritage of the Bouviers, who were supposedly descended from a 16th-century French nobleman, was sheer invention, cooked up by Jackie's paternal grandfather in the 1920s. Jackie's father, John Vernou Bouvier III, had a seat on the New York Stock Exchange, an apartment on Park Avenue and, during much of his life, debts that exceeded his assets. Devilishly handsome, "Black Jack" Bouvier was a social meteor who left behind him a swath of female conquests and empty champagne bottles. He conducted affairs with his wife's friends, using the groundskeeper's shack on the ninth hole of his country

The Bouviers

Jacqueline Bouvier, 14, in East Hampton, New York, with her adored father, "Black Jack", and her doting paternal grandfather, John Vernou Bouvier Jr. When "Grampy Jack" died five years later, in 1948, the family was stunned to discover that he had spent the bulk of his fortune. Jackie inherited a mere $3,000.

HAMMERSMITH FARM

Hammersmith Farm, on the outskirts of Newport, Rhode Island, dates to the seventeenth century, when King Charles I of England gave the property to one of his surveyors, William Brenton. The 28-room "cottage" where Jacqueline Bouvier spent her summers as a teenager was built much later, in 1887, by the first member of the Auchincloss family to own the land. Jackie loved the house with its romantic sunken garden, designed by Frederick Law Olmsted. During summertime stays at Hammersmith, she rode horses and did farm chores, collecting eggs from the henhouse. In 1953 Jackie chose Hammersmith Farm as the setting for her wedding reception, tossing her bridal bouquet from the staircase in the main hall.

Horses, to which Jack was allergic, and elegant garden parties were regular features of life at Hammersmith Farm. By Auchincloss standards, the Kennedy women, with their trendy outfits and streaked hair, were *nouveaux riches*, and Irish politicos from Boston were as exotic as characters out of the musical *Guys and Dolls*.

Jack Kennedy paid numerous visits to Hammersmith, and after he became president his in-laws, the Auchinclosses, would move to an older home on the property to make room in the main house for his entourage. While Jack enjoyed sipping daiquiris on the deck with its spectacular view of Narragansett Bay, the charm of vacationing on a working farm eluded him. He once complained to Secret Service agent Larry Newman that there was nothing to do but watch a lot of ponies run around in the yard.

An accomplished equestrienne, Jackie brought her own horse, Danseuse, with her to Miss Porter's School and regularly won prizes in competitions. She continued riding as an adult (above), and as first lady spent several days a week at Glen Ora, the Kennedys' leased estate in Virginia hunt country.

club golf course for mid-afternoon assignations. As a broker, he had specialized in stock pools during the days before SEC regulations—but unlike Joe Kennedy, he often lost money.

Janet Lee Bouvier separated from Black Jack for the first time when Jackie was seven and divorced him four years later. Janet soon remarried, taking as her second husband Hugh D. Auchincloss, a gentle, utterly conventional man with a speech impediment who owned magnificent estates in McLean, Virginia, and Newport, Rhode Island. "Hughdie" tolerated Janet's constant chatter. "To speak to your mother is to interrupt her," he once remarked to their son, Jamie. He was also kind to his stepchildren, who included the future novelist Gore Vidal, a legacy from an earlier marriage. In Jackie's eyes, however, Hughdie could not compete with Black Jack Bouvier, who took her to see the thoroughbreds race at Belmont Park and treated her to pistachio ice cream at Schrafft's, the favorite soda fountain of Manhattan's pre-teen set.

Amazingly enough, Jackie Bouvier was not considered attractive as a girl. Big-boned and rangy in an era when petite women were the ideal, she had mannish hands and large feet that eventually grew to fill size ten-and-a-half shoes. Her hair

was frizzy, her complexion problematic, and her unusually wide-set eyes were thought to be a defect. As a teenager, Jackie worked hard to make herself over, cultivating a breathy, little-girl voice in order to compensate for her size. Her efforts succeeded so brilliantly that in 1948 society columnist Igor Cassini, Oleg's brother, who wrote under the name Clolly Knickerbocker, anointed her as "Queen Debutante of the Year 1947." Jackie went on to study French literature at Vassar and the Sorbonne, and in 1951 she won *Vogue* magazine's Prix de Paris competition. Her submission, chosen over 1,280 other entries, included an essay on three historical figures she would like to have known. Jackie's choices—Oscar Wilde, Charles Baudelaire, and Serge Diaghilev—reflected her rarefied sensibility.

The first prize in the competition was a year's internship divided between *Vogue's* offices in New York and Paris. Jackie quit the internship after just a few days. There are varying accounts of why she left what was considered a debutante's dream job, but at the time her parents were competing for her attention. Black Jack very much wanted his daughter to live in New York. Janet was equally determined to have her in Washington, where she would be nearer to Merrywood, the Auchincloss estate. Janet won, and Jackie became yet another of the good-looking women who got hired by the *Times-Herald* on the strength of a recommendation from Arthur Krock, who happened to be an old friend of Hughdie's.

Jack was running for the Senate in 1952 and he was also dating three other women besides Jackie, so it seems unlikely that the courting couple spent a great deal of time together. Whether consciously or not, Jackie allowed herself to fall in love with a man who had Black Jack Bouvier's glamour, with considerably more substance but also the same penchant for infidelity. From Jack's point of view, he had found a woman who was a sparkling conversationalist, highly intelligent, and—critically important—capable of passing muster with his father. Reared as a Catholic, Jackie was an interesting combination of sophistication and innocence. She had been engaged for a short time to a New York stockbroker named John Husted, who later described their relationship as "chaste." On the other hand, Jackie was used to managing older men with active libidos and Joe did not intimidate her. She seemed to genuinely enjoy his company, and impressed him with her wicked sense of humor and passion for gossip.

Jackie got along less well with Jack's sisters and sister-in-law, Ethel. Visiting Hyannis Port, she was appalled to see the women roughhousing on the lawn and even more dismayed to learn that she was expected to take part in the Kennedys' famous games of touch football. When not competing, the Kennedy

Life in Hyannis Port
After proclaiming John F. Kennedy the Senate's most eligible bachelor, the media treated the announcement of his engagement as major news. In June 1953, *Life* magazine photographers followed Jackie on a visit with her future in-laws in Hyannis Port, even capturing shots of Jackie and Jack out for a recreational sail.

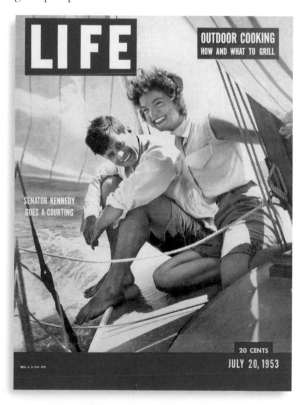

A NICE TRADITIONAL LAMPSHADE

The senator and his bride emerged from Saint Mary's Church to face a clutch of press photographers and a crowd of 3,000 curious spectators.

Jacqueline Bouvier got her first taste of political life when it came time to select her wedding gown. Her preference was for a sleek, contemporary look, but Jack, knowing that press photographers would be out in force, asked her to "wear something traditional." Jackie settled on a dress favored by her mother, whose design featured an elaborate shirred bodice and a full skirt decorated with multiple tiers of ruffles. She also wore an antique lace veil, a family heirloom. The wedding made the front page of the *New York Times*, but Jackie later confided to her daughter Caroline that she had never liked that fussy wedding dress. "It reminded me of a lampshade," she said.

women interrogated Jackie about her personal life and teased her mercilessly with pointed remarks about everything from the size of her feet to her preference for the French pronunciation of her given name—Jackleen, with a soft J. Kennedys were expected to take such ribbing and dole it out with gusto. Constant teasing undoubtedly created the leathery egos that served the Kennedys well in the political arena, but it was hard on a woman of refined sensibilities.

Whether she liked it or not, Jackie soon realized that she was marrying the entire Kennedy clan, not to mention Jack's career. The formal announcement of the couple's engagement, in June 1953, had to be delayed because the *Saturday Evening Post* was about to publish a profile entitled "Jack Kennedy—the Senate's Gay Young Bachelor." Jackie and Janet's preference for a relatively informal wedding was also overruled, this time by the father-in-law to be. At Joe's insistence, the Catholic ceremony on September 12 was followed by a lavish reception at Hammersmith Farm, the Auchinclosses' Newport estate, attended by more than 1,300 guests. The Kennedy clan arrived en masse, seriously overdressed by Auchincloss standards. One friend of the bride's family recalled with a shudder the presence of a large number of Boston-area political types—large, ruddy-faced men in electric blue suits.

Black Jack Bouvier had been slated to give the bride away. Inordinately fond of his daughter, but also nervous about confronting his hostile ex-wife and her friends, Black Jack soothed his nerves with whiskey. On the morning of the ceremony, he was found drunk in his hotel room. Janet, in no mood to be embarrassed one more time, banned him from the church, and Jackie walked down the aisle on the arm of her stepfather. Terribly disappointed, Jackie accepted the situation with such aplomb that even members of the wedding party were unaware of the reasons for the switch until much later.

Although Jackie knew about her groom's reputation, she was also young enough to believe in the reforming power of love. Within months of the wedding, Jack had returned to his old habits, and Jackie campaigned for his attention by attempting to transform herself into the perfect courtesan/wife. She upgraded Jack's diet as well as his wardrobe. (Miserly about some things,

he had been in the habit of ordering cheap suits, which he never got around to having fitted.) Jackie took college classes in American history and political science, as well as lessons in bridge, golf, and French cooking. She was good at games and a natural athlete, but her attempt at turning out a gourmet dinner on the cook's night off produced only overdone chops, scorched chocolate sauce, and coffee heated so long that there was nothing left but a burned pot.

A more serious blow to Jackie's confidence was the miscarriage she suffered in 1954. Considering the emphasis that the Kennedys placed on having many children—Jack talked of having five—the absence of a baby in the house constituted a family crisis and a serious blow to her self-esteem. To make matters worse, the young couple almost never had time alone. Their vacations and weekend getaways were invariably spent in Palm Beach or Hyannis Port, where Jackie opted out of the scheduled activities in order to sit by herself, reading a book. Jackie was moody and restless. Jack, meanwhile, was expanding his roster of girlfriends. By 1955, he was seeing a six-foot-tall burlesque dancer named Tempest Storm, as well as a Radcliffe student and sometime Washington intern who was still in her teens.

A Perfect Wedding

The large wedding party included Jackie's sister Lee as matron of honor, her stepsister Nina Auchincloss as maid of honor, eight bridesmaids, a flower girl, a page, and 14 groomsmen. Jackie's bouquet of orchids carried out the pink and white color scheme, and guests—who had arrived at the reception in some 500 cars—danced to the music of Meyer Davis's society orchestra.

Author and Candidate
1954–1960

With his marriage already under stress, Jack Kennedy was also wrestling with an issue that could have profound consequences for his political future. The Senate was debating a motion to censure Wisconsin Republican Joe McCarthy. Failure to vote for censure would seriously damage Jack's standing with the liberal wing of his party. But McCarthy was a hero to many of his state's Irish Catholic voters, and he also happened to be a personal friend. Eunice Kennedy had dated McCarthy for a while during a period when she and Jack were sharing a town house in Georgetown, and she later served as a bridesmaid at McCarthy's 1953 wedding to Jean Kerr. Joe Kennedy had contributed to McCarthy's campaign fund. Bobby, meanwhile, briefly served as general counsel on McCarthy's subcommittee. A bitter feud soon developed between Bobby and McCarthy's chief aide, Roy Cohn, but Bobby and Ethel thought highly enough of McCarthy to make him the godfather of their daughter Kathleen.

Beginning with the so-called Amerasia scandal, which broke during the closing days of World War II, the American public became aware of charges that the Roosevelt administration had been penetrated by individuals loyal to the Communist Party, some of whom were actively engaged in spying for the Soviet Union. President Harry S. Truman responded by creating a loyalty board system to vet government employees; however, many Democrats remained highly skeptical of the charges that

were emanating from the Federal Bureau of Investigation, and after 1948 the records of loyalty board proceedings were kept confidential. Congress and the public had to take it on faith that the same bureaucrats who created the problem were successfully solving it.

Blunt and aggressive, McCarthy campaigned in 1946 on a promise to get communists off the government payroll. By 1950 he had focused his attention on the State Department, which already had produced both the Amerasia and Alger Hiss espionage cases.

McCarthy was never noted for his depth of research, and his tendency to improvise his speeches made him vulnerable to charges that he was engaged in a partisan witch-hunt. He, in turn, interpreted personal attacks as evidence that his critics were engaged in a cover-up and responded by ratcheting up his rhetoric, talking about an "immense" conspiracy that encompassed virtually the entire Democratic Party. By 1952, Jack could no longer support McCarthy's tactics, though he was even more worried that liberal Democrats would be successful in convincing the public that "McCarthyism" was more dangerous than communism.

Jack's feelings became abundantly clear during a Spee Club reunion banquet at Harvard held in February 1952. When an after-dinner speaker remarked that he was proud Harvard had never graduated an Alger Hiss and even prouder that it had never produced a Joe McCarthy, Jack exploded in anger. Rising at his seat, he shouted, "How dare you couple the name of a great American patriot with that of a traitor!" This was a rare outburst from a man who prided himself on his cool, cerebral approach to policy questions. The other diners lapsed into shocked silence, and Jack departed without hearing the rest of the program.

By the time the motion to censure McCarthy was introduced in 1954, the Wisconsin senator was drinking heavily and had blundered into a pointless investigation of the U.S. Army that increasingly looked like a personal vendetta on the part of his aides, Cohn and G. David Schine. Jack had no doubt that his old friend had gone too far, but he also hoped to limit the political damage to a cause he still believed in. Joining with anti-communist liberals Hubert H. Humphrey and Wayne Morse, he sponsored the Communist Control Act, which in its original form would have made membership in the Communist Party USA a criminal offense. Meanwhile, with the help of Ted Sorensen, Jack drafted a speech in which he would come out in favor of censure, but only on the limited grounds of Cohn and Schine's handling of the investigation of the Army. The text of the speech made a

Senator Joe

Like many old friends of Joe McCarthy (above), Jack blamed the Wisconsin Senator's descent into conspiracy-mongering on his aide, Roy Cohn. He also worried that the furor over "McCarthyism" was, in part, a cynical attempt to discredit the anti-communist cause.

point of observing that Jack still supported McCarthy's "views and objectives in years gone by."

This speech was never delivered. The censure motion was still bottled up in committee in October, when Jack entered the Hospital for Special Surgery in New York, where doctors performed a complicated two-part operation to fuse sections of his spinal vertebrae. Since the previous spring, he had been using crutches most of the time, and by late summer walking had become so painful that he remained at his desk on the Senate floor between votes. Jack's personal physician, Dr. Sara Jordan of the Lahey Clinic, had warned that Addison's disease made any surgery risky, but Jack found the prospect of life as an invalid, perhaps confined to a wheelchair, too depressing to contemplate. As in the past, Jack came out of the operation well, only to suffer a relapse a few days later. This time, he contracted a urinary tract infection so massive that he fell into a coma and was near death.

Before the severity of his condition was known, wags in the capital had speculated that the operation was conveniently timed to rescue Senator Kennedy from having to take sides for or against McCarthy. This wasn't so. However, when the Senate finally did vote in December on a watered-down motion to condemn— not censure—McCarthy, Jack was recuperating in the hospital, and he did not bother to pair his vote with another non-voting senator. His inaction had no effect on the fate of the motion, which passed by a three-to-one majority, but he was the only Democratic senator who failed to go on record against McCarthy.

Jack's surgical wound refused to heal, and he spent the early part of 1955 recuperating at his parents' house in Palm Beach, briefly returning to New York in February for surgery to remove a metal plate that had been implanted during the first operation. On May 24, he returned to the Senate, celebrating the occasion by walking unaided up the Capitol steps in full view of news photographers. Despite this demonstration, he was still in agony. On weekends he quietly slipped out of Washington for unpublicized hospital stays at New York Hospital, where he received treatment from yet another specialist, Dr. Janet Travell, who administered Novocain injections in conjunction with physical therapy.

THE KENNEDY ROCKING CHAIR

Once JFK gave them his stamp of approval, rocking chairs were no longer just for the elderly.

Over the years, Kennedy tried many strategies to avoid back strain. He slept with a board under his mattress and wore a lift in his left shoe to compensate for a disparity in the length of his legs. In 1955 he consulted Dr. Janet Travell, who suggested that using a rocking chair might provide gentle exercise for the muscles in his lower back. Kennedy purchased a simple Appalachian oak rocker for $30 from the P & P Company, a North Carolina manufacturer. Kennedy became so attached to the chair that, as president, he took it with him when he traveled on Air Force One. He also placed copies of the chair at Camp David, at his home in Hyannis Port, and at the Kennedy house in Palm Beach, and gave still other chairs as gifts to friends. The proliferation of "authentic" Kennedy rockers would later lead to some confusion as several examples turned up on the auction block.

Bored during his months of enforced bed rest, Jack had conceived the idea for a book about U.S. senators who had risked their political careers by taking unpopular stands in defense of the national interest as they saw it. He solicited suggestions from friends and staff members, coming up with a list that ranged from John Quincy Adams and Daniel Webster to Robert Taft, the conservative Republican from Ohio. With the possible exception of the first and last chapters of the manuscript, which Jack may have drafted, the book was written largely by Jack's able aide Sorensen, who had ghosted articles for him in the past. Sorensen was assisted by Professor Jules Davids of Georgetown University, whose course in American history Jackie had audited.

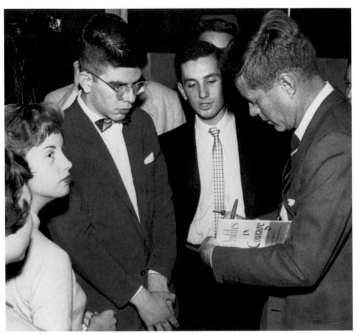

Profiles in Courage appeared in early 1956 and quickly became a best-seller, thanks in part to lavish promotion and the appearance of pre-publication excerpts in variety of periodicals, ranging from *Reader's Digest* to *Harper's*. Joe Kennedy once again sent his agents into key bookstores to purchase thousands of copies. Arthur Krock, meanwhile, wrote letters to members of the Pulitzer prize advisory board, urging them to consider Jack's book

Senatorial Signing

Sen. Kennedy autographs his Pulitzer prize–winning book for a youthful admirer. While *Profiles in Courage* may have been the work of many hands, it was also an expression of Jack Kennedy's belief in the power of idealism working within the traditions of democracy.

for the most prestigious award available to a nonfiction author. Krock's efforts bore fruit. Although the panel of scholarly judges took no notice of *Profiles in Courage*, the advisory board ignored their nominations and awarded the book the prize for the year's best biography. Ironically, Sen. John F. Kennedy was now famous for celebrating political courage, even though he himself had dodged his most critical test, finding a discreet silence to be the better part of valor.

It was by no means uncommon for an elected official to rely on ghostwriters. Jack's claim to be the sole author of *Profiles in Courage* only began to raise serious ethical questions when he accepted literary accolades and used them to burnish his reputation as a deep thinker and accomplished writer. Washington was rife with speculation, but anyone who dared to suggest that Jack had taken too much credit came in for harsh treatment from the Kennedy camp. When columnist Drew Pearson called *Profiles* ghostwritten during a televised interview, he received a stern letter from Washington attorney Clark Clifford, who pressured him into issuing a retraction. Even the FBI got into the act. Possibly at the instigation of Joe Kennedy, the bureau launched an investigation of a group of New York literary figures who were talking about protesting the Pulitzer board's decision.

Interestingly enough, Jack was genuinely indignant over the charge that he had relied on a ghostwriter. He would later complain bitterly to Arthur Krock

about the persistent rumors, recalling how he had struggled to write while confined to bed, in pain from his spinal surgery. The Kennedy Library eventually compiled eight folders of handwritten pages, along with some tapes of Jack's dictation, as evidence of his authorship. However, biographer Herbert S. Parmet, who studied this material in detail, concluded that Jack was at best the "overseer" of the project. Presumably, Jack was so accustomed to relying on his staff that he couldn't quite grasp that other authors didn't work this way.

In 1956, meanwhile, pro-Kennedy operatives succeeded in wresting control of the Massachusetts Democratic organization, throwing its support to Adlai Stevenson, the party's likely nominee for the presidency. Jack's reward was an opportunity to narrate a campaign film called *The Pursuit of Happiness* that had been produced by former MGM production chief Dore Schary for screening on the opening night of the Democratic convention in Chicago. His performance was so charismatic that it nearly swept him into the vice presidential nomination, despite Stevenson's concerns that Jack's youth and religion would hurt the ticket's chances in November. In the end it was Eleanor Roosevelt who punctured the trial balloon of the Kennedy candidacy, lecturing Jack in front of onlookers for his failure to take a stand against Joe McCarthy.

On an exciting night filled with last-minute maneuvers on the convention floor, Jack narrowly lost the vice presidential nomination on the second ballot to Estes Kefauver of Tennessee. The lesson he took from his near victory was that he didn't have to wait his turn to be anointed by the elder statesmen of the Democratic Party. Given the precarious state of his health, Jack was impatient with the argument that he was too young to run for national office. He was a man in a hurry, determined to seize every opportunity that came his way, and he now saw that he could run for president by appealing directly to party faithful. In essence, his campaign for the 1960 presidential nomination began immediately after the 1956 convention. Though hardly enthusiastic about Adlai Stevenson, he campaigned vigorously for him, using his appearances as an opportunity to build his own name recognition.

The defeat of the Democratic ticket in November scarcely slowed Jack's momentum. Traveling with speechwriter Sorensen, he crisscrossed the country on commercial and chartered airplanes. No occasion was too small to rate a personal appearance by Sen. Kennedy, whether it was a Rotary Club dinner, the dedication of a union hall or an Iowa corn-picking contest. Jack's schedule during these years was exhausting and often

SCRIMSHAW

Some items from JFK's scrimshaw collection featured patriotic themes, such as the Bunker Hill monument, seen above.

Kennedy collected ship models and other artifacts connected with seafaring life. After their marriage, Jackie gave him his first piece of scrimshaw, a small whale's tooth incised with the image of an American ship under full sail. Kennedy gradually acquired other pieces—whale's teeth and walrus tusks bearing distinctive American decorations, including portraits of New Bedford whalers. When he entered the White House, he displayed a few of his favorite examples of scrimshaw on his desk in the Oval Office. And after her husband's death, Mrs. Kennedy placed a small piece of scrimshaw bearing the presidential seal in his coffin. It had been her last Christmas gift to him.

exposed him to physical danger. Sorensen recalled one trip on a small chartered plane when the cabin door was found to be broken and he was assigned to hold it closed for the duration of the flight. On another flight through a driving rainstorm in Alaska, Jack had to reach out the window and manually operate the windshield wipers. By 1959, he had seen his fill of close calls, and formed a corporation to purchase his own Convair airplane, christened the *Caroline* in honor of his baby daughter.

In the Senate, meanwhile, Jack mended fences with the liberal wing of the party by actively fighting for causes like a higher minimum wage. More controversially, he was also serving on the Senate Investigations subcommittee, chaired by Sen. John McClellan of Arkansas. The so-called "McClellan Rackets Committee" was investigating the mob's infiltration of the labor movement. In theory, getting gangsters out of the union halls would benefit workers, but the presence of conservatives like Barry Goldwater on the committee created the danger that the investigation would be seen as an anti-labor exercise. The committee's mission also had ramifications for the Kennedy family. In 1945, Joe had purchased the Chicago Merchandise Mart, at the time the world's largest commercial building, and his plan to transform the enormous space into a complex of wholesalers' showrooms had required an accommodation with gangsters like Sam Giancana, who wielded extensive influence in the unions that kept the mart running. Bobby Kennedy, who served as the committee's chief counsel, would play the more visible role in the investigation. Much to the disgust of his father, he made it his mission to bring down Teamster president Jimmy Hoffa, and he humiliated witness Sam Giancana by accusing him of giggling like a girl. Jack's participation was comparatively low-key, but his effort to pass a major piece of labor reform legislation, with the support of labor leaders Walter Reuther and George Meany, eventually came to nothing.

During this period, Jack also emerged as a spokesman for a more flexible foreign policy. Jack was strongly influenced by the argument that the United States could never win the propaganda war with the worldwide Communist movement as long as it was perceived as a defender of colonialism. Speaking at a St. Patrick's Day rally in Baltimore in 1957, he suggested that the United States take a more active role in aiding the anti-Communist resistance in Eastern European countries like Hungary and Poland. But it should also throw its support behind national liberation movements, such as the struggle against French colonial rule in Algeria. "Whether a man be Hungarian or Irish, Catholic or Moslem, white or black, there forever burns in his breast the unquenchable desire to be free," he declared.

Jack was espousing a position widely considered to be both enlightened and intellectually sophisticated. A few

Jimmy Hoffa

Jack took a political risk by accepting a seat on the McClellan committee, which investigated corrupt labor bosses like Jimmy Hoffa (below) under the direction of its chief counsel, his brother Bobby. The hearings were great theater, but they also won the Kennedy brothers some dangerous enemies.

senior statesmen, including Adlai Stevenson and New York Democrat Herbert Lehman, warned that it was naïve and simplistic to think that terrorist organizations like the Algerian FLN would transform themselves into democratic movements. But such objections seemed almost curmudgeonly in light of Jack's argument that the United States had to stand for something more idealistic than the perpetuation of imperialism. In an article in the magazine *America*, Jack took the position that the longer "legitimate Algerian aspirations" were suppressed, the more likely an eventual communist takeover would become.

Fortunately, during this busy period of Jack's life, both his health and his sometimes rocky marriage had stabilized. Friends and family who had dismissed Jackie as a spoiled debutante were impressed by the way she took care of Jack during his recovery, pitching in to change the bandages that covered her husband's suppurating surgical wound and deftly coping with his irritable outbursts. In the summer of 1956, the marriage suffered another blow. Jackie, who had been seven months pregnant, lost her baby while recuperating at Hammersmith Farm from the hot and often chaotic Chicago convention. Jack, meanwhile, was cruising on a yacht in the Riviera with his Senate colleague George Smathers and, reportedly, one of his numerous girlfriends. When Jackie finally reached her husband three days later, he was initially reluctant to cut short his vacation. He booked passage only after Smathers gave him some pointed advice. "You'd better haul ass back to your wife if you ever want to be president," he said.

Georgetown Years

The Kennedys' home on N Street in the Georgetown section of Washington reflected Jackie's impeccable taste and reserved demeanor. Efforts to portray Jackie in the press as a typical political wife who practiced the domestic arts and scrimped on her clothing budget were unconvincing—and totally unnecessary.

HICKORY HILL

After Jackie's dream house was passed to the Robert Kennedys, it became renowned as a social mecca for Washington insiders.

In 1955 the Kennedys purchased Hickory Hill, a Civil War–era house that had formerly belonged to Supreme Court Justice Robert Jackson. The house was just two miles from Merrywood, where Jackie had lived as a girl. She thought of Hickory Hill as the house where she and Jack would raise a family together, and spent many hours planning the perfect nursery. She also approved designs for special fittings in the master bathroom and dressing room, suited to a man who had to avoid any strain on his lower back.

But a year after Hickory Hill was purchased, Jackie suffered her second miscarriage while vacationing at Hammersmith Farm. Jack was cruising on the Riviera, reportedly in the company of a socialite known as "Pooh," and in no hurry to return home to comfort his wife. Her dreams of a picture-book family dashed, Jackie couldn't bear to live at Hickory Hill again. Jack then sold the house to his brother Robert.

The widely circulated rumor that Joe Kennedy paid Jackie $1 million to stay with his son dates from this period. There was no payoff, but Joe did purchase a townhouse for Jack and Jackie on N Street in Georgetown, a replacement for their Virginia home, Hickory Hill, which Jackie had renovated in the hope of raising a large family and now found unbearably depressing. In November 1957, Jackie gave birth to a healthy daughter, Caroline. With the arrival of Caroline, Jack's emotional defenses seemed to melt away. For the first time, he took genuine delight in his family.

Under other circumstances, Caroline's birth might have caused Jack to become a more faithful husband. But his grueling schedule kept him away from home most of the time and allowed him to continue to compartmentalize his conscience. Like many political wives before and since, Jackie found that she had little leverage. If she decided to leave her husband, she would very likely destroy his chances of becoming president and be shunned by his friends and supporters as a vengeful and selfish woman. Jackie wasn't prepared to take such drastic action. In the end, she followed the same path that Rose had chosen decades earlier. She kept her own counsel, carved out an independent routine, and took out her frustrations by running up bills for designer gowns and antique furniture.

Jack complained about his wife's spendthrift habits, though considering the millions that Joe Kennedy was spending to further his son's political ambitions, Jackie's budget was hardly out of line. Long before any official announcement, Jack was already assembling a presidential campaign organization. In addition to Bobby Kennedy and Stephen Smith, who was married to Jack's sister Jean, his chief strategists were Kenny O'Donnell and Larry O'Brien, the most important of a group of Massachusetts-based staffers who came to be known jokingly as "the Murphia," or Irish Mafia. The organization quietly began to conduct polls and do research on likely delegates to the 1960 nominatory convention. Bobby, who had not yet joined the campaign full-time, accepted speaking engagements in the South, where his role as the nemesis of Jimmy Hoffa made him a popular figure. Jack also made campaign contributions to Democratic candidates around the country.

At the 1958 Gridiron dinner, an annual event where members of the Washington press corps roasted politicians with satirical skits, Jack was serenaded to the tune of "My Heart Belongs to Daddy," whose lyrics had been changed to "Send the bill to daddy." Jack took the teasing in good humor. In his response to the skit, he read a telegram allegedly from his father: "Dear Jack," it said, "Don't buy a single vote more than is necessary— I'll be damned if I'm going to pay for a landslide."

Jack Kennedy's approach to running for president has now become commonplace: A would-be candidate spends a private fortune to build his own organization and enter numerous state primaries. But on January 2, 1960, when Jack officially announced his candidacy, the situation was far different. The leading contenders for the Democratic nomination were Senate Majority Leader Lyndon Johnson and Senator Stuart Symington of Missouri. Adlai Stevenson also had a following, despite having lost twice to Eisenhower. None of the three was planning to campaign actively in the primaries. State laws differed, but many such contests were dominated by favorite-son candidates, locally prominent politicians who would have the power to broker their votes on the convention floor.

Kennedy entered eight primaries but faced significant opposition only in Wisconsin and West Virginia, where he ran against Sen. Hubert H. Humphrey. Known as the "Happy Warrior," Humphrey was the most liberal candidate in

Kennedy and King

Candidate Kennedy greets black voters in 1960. The reverend Martin Luther King Sr. had endorsed Nixon while his son, the 31-year-old civil rights leader, chose to remain officially neutral. When King Jr. was arrested in Atlanta, the Democratic governor of Georgia promised to secure his release if Kennedy would refrain from publicly condemning the arrest. Kennedy agreed but made a personal call to Mrs. King, expressing his sympathy.

Favorite Son

Jack's narration of a campaign film on the opening night of the 1956 Democratic National Convention was followed by a demonstration organized by Massachusetts delegates. The crowd's enthusiastic response almost catapulted him into the second spot on the ticket. In the end, Jack was passed over in favor of Estes Kefauver of Tennessee, but the demonstration (right) marked the unofficial beginning of his campaign for the 1960 presidential nomination.

Jackie Campaigns

Though often amused by politics as a subject, Jackie was far from a natural at the daily grind of campaigning. The voters loved her anyway, and her ability to speak fluent Italian and French was a tremendous asset in ethnic neighborhoods.

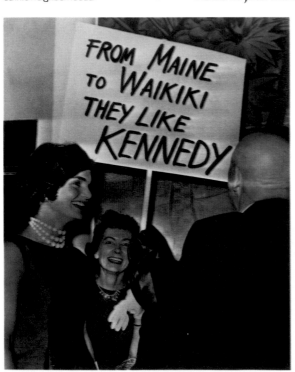

the race and beloved by organized labor. The view inside the Kennedy camp was that Humphrey had no chance to win the nomination, but if he carried either state it would destroy Jack's hope of arriving at the convention with "the endorsement of the people."

Wisconsin, next door to Humphrey's home state of Minnesota, was not the battleground Jack would have chosen. But the Kennedy organization was much superior to Humphrey's relatively amateurish effort. On Election Day, Jack pulled 56 percent of the vote, although his relatively poor showing among Protestants did not bode well for West Virginia, where only five percent of the population was Catholic and the Humphrey organization had chosen as its theme song "Give Me That Old Time Religion."

Depending on one's point of view, the religious question was either sheer bigotry or the reflection of a legitimate concern that a Catholic president would follow the Vatican's positions on social issues and aid to parochial schools. In the final days of the campaign, Franklin Roosevelt Jr., whose name was still revered by West Virginia coal miners, arrived to conduct a televised interview in which Jack addressed the subject head-on, stating, "I would not take orders from any pope, cardinal, bishop, or priest. Nor would they try to give me orders." Such behavior, he added, would be "a sin against God" as well as grounds for impeachment. As Ted Sorensen would later observe, Jack had succeeded in turning the issue around. West Virginia voters were now "anxious to disprove the charge of bigotry" and Jack scored a decisive victory, carrying 61 percent of the vote.

As far as Jack was concerned, religion was just another area of life that he had successfully relegated to its own compartment. When the Vatican newspaper *L'Osservatore Romano* unhelpfully stated that the church did indeed have both "the duty and the right" to tell Catholic officeholders how to vote, Jack was surprised and exasperated. "Now I understand why Henry VIII set up his own church," he groused to his aides.

The "Murphia" was not afraid to confront the religion issue, but they did worry about their candidate's wife. Fearful that voters would be put off by Jackie's little-girl voice and upper-class background, they were hesitant to give her a prominent role in the campaign. It was true that Jackie was ill at ease making small talk with "ordinary" people. She did not know any recipes for Jell-o Salad. Nevertheless, when asked to pitch in, Jackie was a trouper. She gamely positioned herself in front of the cash registers at supermarkets, shaking hands with customers even as she silently commiserated with the attempts of some shoppers to avoid her. Despite the efforts of Jack's advisors, who did their best to hide the existence

KENNEDY ON THE LINKS

Jack Kennedy relaxes with a round of golf in Hyannis Port.

Despite his recurring back problems, Kennedy enjoyed the game of golf. But during his campaign for the presidency, this became a sensitive issue. Eisenhower had been widely criticized for spending too much time on the golf course, and JFK's aides did their best to keep the press from running stories about their candidate's golfing habit. Later, as president, Kennedy had to contend with warnings from his doctors, who feared that he would aggravate his spinal problems. Unworried, he invited reporters to watch him tee off, demonstrating the idiosyncratic swing he'd developed to avoid straining his back muscles. When items from Jacqueline Kennedy Onassis's estate were auctioned in 1996, Jack's golf clubs were among the stars of the event. His MacGregor woods, valued at $900, fetched $772,500. His set of Ben Hogan irons were sold for $387,500, and the winning bid for his putter was $67,750.

of Caroline's nanny Maud Smith, it is doubtful that the public mistook Jackie for a typical housewife. Still, most were charmed by Jackie's youth, beauty and soft-spoken manner.

Just as Jack's staff was beginning to realize her value, Jackie discovered that she was pregnant again. Fearful of a third miscarriage, she retired from active campaigning. In July, when the Democratic delegates gathered in Los Angeles, Jackie stayed in Hyannis Port, watching the convention on television.

Although momentum was strongly in his favor, Jack was far from having a majority of the delegates committed to him. As the proceedings got under way in Los Angeles, the apparently moribund Stevenson and Johnson campaigns suddenly sprang to life. Demonstrators loyal to Adlai, the sentimental favorite, marched outside the Sports Arena, and Eleanor Roosevelt and Hubert Humphrey threw their support his way. Ex-president Harry Truman, known for saying exactly what was on his mind, gave a televised press conference in which he declared that Jack—whom he mistakenly or otherwise referred to as "Joeseph"—was too young and immature to be president. Meanwhile, Adam Clayton Powell, the Harlem Democratic leader, announced for Lyndon Johnson, and India Edwards, the chairman of Citizens for Johnson, pointedly reminded reporters of Senator Kennedy's history of poor health. Edwards became the first person to say publicly that John F. Kennedy had Addison's disease and was dependent on daily doses of cortisone.

The Kennedys had consistently lied about Jack's condition, and this was hardly the moment to confess the truth. The family's official position, articulated by Jack in a 1959 interview, was that he did not have classical Addison's but merely a "partial adrenal insufficiency." The slim justification for this statement was that Jack had not contracted Addison's as the result of having tuberculosis, once thought to be the most common cause of the condition. Responding to Edwards' comments, Bobby Kennedy and Ted Sorensen compounded this deception by flatly denying that the senator was taking cortisone.

As a result of such denials, Jack came under pressure to demonstrate his stamina by following an exhausting schedule that was arguably more

demanding than necessary. Within a few months Chuck Spalding, an old friend, recommended the services of Dr. Max Jacobson, a notorious quack who injected his celebrity patients with B12 cocktails laced with methamphetamine. Jack and Jackie both began receiving regular injections from Jacobson, a practice that continued after the election.

The flurry of last-minute attacks failed to erode Kennedy's momentum, and on Wednesday evening, July 13, he was nominated on the first ballot. But the Kennedy camp scarcely had time to savor their victory before it was thrown into disarray over Jack's choice of a running mate. It was generally assumed that Symington of Missouri was the leading contender for the vice presidential nomination. Moreover, Bobby Kennedy had specifically promised key supporters like Walter Reuther and New York Liberal Party leader Alex Rose that Lyndon Johnson would not be chosen.

Johnson did have his advocates in the Kennedy camp, including Joe Kennedy, who thought that he could help the ticket in the South and reassure critics who complained that Jack was too young and inexperienced. The conventional wisdom, however, was that Johnson would never give up his post as Senate majority leader for the relatively powerless job of vice president. Apparently, Jack decided to offer Johnson the second spot on the ticket as a conciliatory gesture that would mollify both the powerful senator and his own father. Once Johnson turned the job down, he would be free to pick the running mate of his choice.

But when Jack spoke with Johnson in his hotel suite Thursday morning, the Texan did not decline as expected. After asking for time to think the offer over, Johnson decided to accept for the good of the Party. Later, Johnson confessed to Clare Boothe Luce that his change of heart wasn't entirely unselfish. He had consulted a reference book and found that one out of four presidents died in office. "I'm a gamblin' man, darlin'," he told Luce.

The Kennedys were stunned by this turn of events. With Jack's permission, Bobby went to see Johnson and suggested, none too subtly, that by accepting the nomination he would throw the convention into turmoil and hurt the Democrats' chances in November. Needless to say, Johnson was furious. Refusing to continue the conversation, he phoned Jack, demanding to know where he stood. At this point,

FEAT OF CLAY

At the 1960 Summer Olympics in Rome, 18-year-old boxer Cassius Clay (later known as Muhammed Ali) won the gold medal by defeating Polish star Ziggy Pietrzykowski.

Canines for Kennedy
In a lighter moment of the 1960 campaign, a Democratic dachshund toes the party line. Nixon's 1952 speech, invoking his wife's "respectable Republican cloth coat" and humble cocker spaniel, Checkers, as testaments to his financial integrity was a great success at the time, but Democrats relentlessly mocked "the Checkers speech" as an example of Nixon's tendency toward mawkish self-pity.

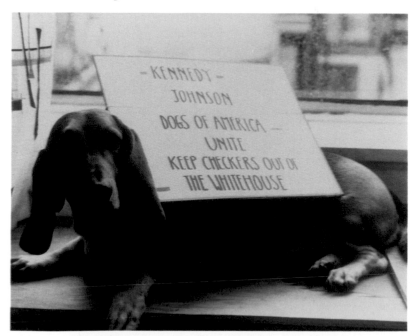

Jack must have realized that he could not withdraw an invitation that had already been accepted. Word was bound to get out, humiliating Johnson and splitting the party.

On the final night of the convention, Jack delivered a ringing acceptance speech on the theme of the "New Frontier." His campaign, he announced, would not be about "what I intend to offer the American people but what I intend to ask of them." Appealing to his listeners' sense of national pride and spirit of sacrifice, he called on Americans to accept the challenge of promoting scientific progress and space exploration, rooting out pockets of prejudice and poverty, and finding solutions to the "unsolved problems of peace and war."

Jack's words had little immediate impact. The clumsy handling of the vice presidential nomination had left all factions of the party feeling betrayed, if for different reasons. Associated Press commentator James Marlow summed up the mood of the convention, noting that the response to the nominee was "the least enthusiastic of the past sixteen years." The reason, in Marlow's opinion, was "that it is difficult to get emotional about a technician."

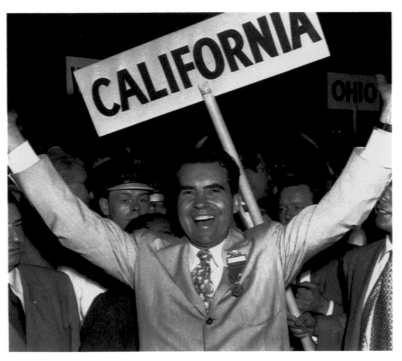

A Close Call

Richard Nixon campaigned energetically in his home state, but at 2 A.M. on election night, California's 32 electoral votes still hung in the balance. At noon that day, Nixon's press secretary conceded the state to Kennedy. Days later, it became apparent that the concession had been premature: Nixon had carried California.

During the course of the general election campaign Jack's friendly relationship with Richard Nixon deteriorated. Still, the two candidates were hard-pressed to define the issues that separated them. Jack eventually resorted to the improbable charge that the Eisenhower administration had been soft on defense. Allegedly, the U.S. had built too few nuclear warheads, allowing the Soviets to open up a "missile gap." The press was rightly skeptical.

During the final weeks of the campaign, opinion polls showed the tide turning in Kennedy's direction, and on Election Day he eked out a narrow victory—capturing 49.7 percent of the popular vote to Nixon's 49.6. This meant that out of almost 69 million ballots cast, just 112,803 more voters had chosen Kennedy. Moreover, while Kennedy would carry the Electoral College by 303 votes to 219, he had won eleven states by less than one percent, often with margins that amounted to a few thousand votes.

At the time, many observers agreed that Kennedy had won because he was, indeed, the better technician. Jack had adopted as his own the maxim of his assistant campaign manager Larry O'Brien, who liked to say that "there is

LAZY-SHAVE

Kennedy and Nixon square during the a televised debate moderated by Howard K. Smith.

John F. Kennedy and Richard Nixon were the first presidential candidates to conduct a series of live televised debates, a tradition that continues to this day. Before the first debate, a member of Nixon's entourage applied a cosmetic called Lazy-Shave to his candidate in an attempt to disguise his five o'clock shadow. Unfortunately, when Nixon began to perspire under the hot studio lights, the Lazy-Shave began to dissolve. Kennedy's more telegenic appearance led to a surge of interest in his campaign, and a few Republican stalwarts, in an effort to suggest that the differences between the two men were entirely cosmetic, charged that Nixon had been "sabotaged" by a makeup artist at the Chicago TV studio. For the second debate Nixon arrived with a new makeup specialist, and he insisted on lowering the temperature of the studio to 70 degrees. Whether or not this was the reason, he gave a better performance, and some critics declared him the winner.

no such thing as too much campaign activity, properly directed." The Kennedy operation's efforts in areas from voter registration and phone banks to public relations raised the ante for future candidates.

Over the years, another view of the Kennedy victory has become prevalent. According to this analysis, Kennedy defeated Nixon because he was more telegenic. There is certainly some truth to this observation. The 1960 campaign was the first to be governed by the rule that good visuals trump verbal content. Audiences who heard the presidential debates between the two candidates over the radio were far more likely to think that Nixon had won than those who watched them on TV. In the television era, theatrical standards were beginning to be applied to real people: Jack Kennedy looked like a leading man. Regardless of what his résumé said, Richard Nixon had been cast by genetics as a character actor.

But looks alone could not explain the Kennedy charisma. After eight years of Eisenhower, the public was in the mood for a change, and Vice President Nixon was in a delicate position when it came to suggesting that a new direction might be in order. Meanwhile, Kennedy's New Frontier theme,

Minnesota Victory
At noon the day after the election, Jack Kennedy learned that he had officially carried Minnesota. With victory now assured, he and Jackie—wearing a coat to disguise her pregnancy—made their appearance at campaign headquarters in Hyannis Port.

which had initially failed to strike sparks among Democratic insiders, gradually caught on. Its rhetoric carefully crafted by Sorensen, the New Frontier was at once an appeal to patriotism and an optimistic vision of social and technological progress. The American Dream was on the verge of full realization, Kennedy proclaimed; citizens just had to be willing to pitch in and do their part.

Among the most fervent believers in the New Frontier were some of the country's leading intellectuals, academics and media opinion makers. Historian Arthur Schlesinger, Jr., for example, wrote that Richard Nixon was in politics to gratify his personal ambition whereas Jack Kennedy had nobler motives. As he put it, "Kennedy is ambitious because the Presidency alone would give him the power to fulfill purposes which have long lain in his mind and heart."

Some of Jack's friends had a more down-to-earth perspective. Benjamin Bradlee, who had covered both sides of the campaign for *Newsweek*, considered Nixon a cipher. The Republican candidate didn't trust the press and rarely let his guard down in the presence of reporters. On the other hand, Bradlee and his wife Tony had socialized with Jack and Jackie in Georgetown, and on election night, even as the final votes were still being counted, they received a call at their Hyannis Port motel summoning them to dinner at the Kennedy compound. Jack started off the evening by glancing at Jackie and Tony, both in the latter stages of pregnancy, and joking, "OK, girls, you can take out the pillows now. We won!"

Later, over dinner, Jack mentioned getting a congratulatory phone call from Mayor Richard Daley of Chicago, who had told him, "Mr. President, with a little bit of luck and the help of a few close friends you're going to carry Illinois." This was a telling anecdote in light of the final Illinois totals. Cook County, the home of Chicago, reported an astounding 89 percent turnout of registered voters, who went for Kennedy by a huge margin of 456,312 votes. Thanks to this overwhelming performance, Jack would carry Illinois by slightly more than 8,000 votes. An Illinois court later barred an official recount, and Mayor Daley brusquely dismissed questions about the improbable result as a "Republican conspiracy." With hindsight, a working journalist might well have been tempted to investigate the story behind Daley's comment, but Bradlee was also understandably reluctant to start down a path that would hurt a personal friend. He rationalized his lack of curiosity by concluding that the Republicans had probably stolen enough votes in southern Illinois to offset whatever may have gone on in Cook County.

With many Republicans calling for recounts, and complaints of election fraud pending in eleven states, Richard Nixon disappointed his supporters by issuing a brief concession statement the following day. In his memoirs, Nixon explained that he was motivated by the fear that "charges of 'sore loser' would follow me through history."

BIRTH OF THE PILL

In 1960 the Food and Drug Administration approved the first oral contraceptive, which used hormones to suppress female egg production. The search for a safe, effective birth-control pill had been promoted by Planned Parenthood since 1956.

Cool Campaigns

In the era before the domination of electronic media, campaign publicity was more creative. Good Humor appealed to voters' partisan appetites by offering a choice between Kennedy and Nixon ice cream bars.

The Torch Is Passed

1961

On January 20, 1961, the nation's capital was transformed. Dwight and Mamie Eisenhower were gone, replaced by a young couple who personified elegance, exuberant high spirits, and cutting-edge fashion. Not even a storm that dumped eight inches of snow on the city could dampen the celebratory mood. Frank Sinatra had kicked off the festivities by hosting an inaugural eve gala with appearances by an all-star cast, including Ella Fitzgerald, Bette Davis, and Jimmy Durante. The inaugural ceremony proper featured contralto Marian Anderson singing the national anthem and the venerable poet Robert Frost—who found that the noonday glare made it impossible to read the poem he had penned for the occasion but saved the moment by reciting another of his works, "The Gift Outright."

Inauguration Day 1961 produced a series of memorable images: the 43-year-old president defying the cold by arriving for the ceremony without a hat or overcoat; Jacqueline Kennedy, just 31, inspiring a fashion trend with her Oleg Cassini coat and Halston pillbox hat; and a lavish inaugural parade with more than forty floats, including an actual Navy PT boat mounted on a truck bed, all dedicated to the theme "World Peace through New Frontiers."

But the 35th president's inaugural address was by no means overshadowed. Less than 1,400 words long, the speech was crafted mainly by Ted Sorensen but reflected Jack Kennedy's lifelong admiration for the prose of Winston Churchill, a master at piling

one ringing phrase upon another until he had scaled the Himalayas of rhetoric. In contrast to most such speeches, this one was not addressed to Americans but to the world at large. The text called for civility and cooperation to achieve scientific progress and eliminate poverty, but for the most part it was a proclamation of intent to win the cold war:

"Let the word go forth from this time and place, to friend and foe alike, that the torch has been passed to a new generation of Americans, born in this century, tempered by war, disciplined by a hard and bitter peace, proud of our ancient heritage, and unwilling to witness or permit the slow undoing of those human rights to which this nation has always been committed, and to which we are committed today at home and around the world."

In one of the few sentences in which he did speak directly to the nation, the new president made no promises but called for sacrifice:

"And so, my fellow Americans, ask not what your country can do for you; ask what you can do for your country."

THE FITZGERALD BIBLE

The Fitzgerald family Bible includes a page of handwritten entries, chronicling important genealogical events, among them the birth of JFK.

Kennedy's inauguration on January 20, 1961, marked the first time a United States president had sworn the oath of office on a Roman Catholic Bible. The Bible used on this occasion was a Fitzgerald family heirloom, said to have been brought from Ireland by Kennedy's maternal ancestors. It arrived from Boston in a Supreme supermarket shopping bag, carried by Rose Kennedy's younger brother. An 1850 Douay English translation, the Bible includes pages of handwritten notes listing marriages, births and deaths, the first of which records the marriage of JFK's great-grandparents, Tom and Rosie [Rosanna] Fitzgerald. The Bible was later donated by the family to the John Fitzgerald Kennedy Library.

In keeping with this grand beginning, the new administration exuded energy and optimism. There are two kinds of U.S. presidents, those who have previous experience running a large enterprise and those who do not. Eisenhower had belonged to the first category, and when he met with his successor during the transition, he talked about organizing the president's staff to create clear lines of responsibility. Eisenhower warned that every American president spent most of his time coping with crises and had no time to oversee the workings of the executive branch as a whole. Jack was unimpressed. He envisioned himself exercising a more personal style of leadership via people he knew and trusted. His appointees tended to be men who lacked established political constituencies; in quite a few cases, they also lacked experience or well developed policy ideas. For the key post of attorney general, Jack chose his brother Bobby, a lawyer who had never tried a case.

On the domestic front, the aura of youthful vigor that surrounded the new first couple was something of a façade. Less than three weeks after the election, on November 25, Jackie had given birth to a son, John F. Kennedy, Jr. The baby was almost a month premature, and the difficult caesarean delivery left her physically debilitated, suffering from "tension headaches," a.k.a. migraines, and depression. It took a Dexedrine pill provided by White House physician Janet Travell to rouse her from bed to attend the inaugural balls. In photographs taken that night, Jackie was dazzling, but she made an appearance at only two of the five balls.

JACKIE'S SIGNATURE STYLE

The new president and first lady arriving at the Washington Armory Inaugural Ball. Jackie's gown earned rave reviews, but the strain she was under shows in her face. Exhausted and still recovering from a difficult delivery, she had roused herself from bed to dress for the gala event.

Under pressure from her husband and his aides to wear American-made clothes on important occasions, Jackie Kennedy asked Oleg Cassini, an American designer for Hollywood films, to dress her for the inauguration. Cassini created an A-line, sable-trimmed coat that Jackie wore with a matching pillbox hat. The coat's three-quarter length sleeves, oversize buttons, and knee-length hem suggested a little girl dressing up in sophisticated clothes, a look that emphasized the youthfulness of the incoming administration. Although both the coat and pillbox hat would be much copied, the most talked about costume of the week was the white peau d'ange sheath with matching floor-length cape that Jackie wore to the Inaugural balls. She had designed the ensemble herself and had it made up at the custom shop of the Bergdorf Goodman department store in New York.

TV TOURS THE WHITE HOUSE

On Valentine's Day 1962, CBS and NBC aired a special tour of the White House conducted by Jacqueline Kennedy. The first lady had announced her plans to mount a restoration of the White House a year earlier, explaining to journalist Hugh Sidey that her goal was to transform the president's home into a historical monument, filled with authentic period rooms and genuine antiques. She called the project "a question of scholarship," adding, "It would be a sacrilege merely to decorate—a word I hate."

Americans responded by donating more than $10

Jackie welcomes CBS correspondent Charles Collingwood—and the TV audience—to the White House.

million worth of family heirlooms, including five rare early nineteenth-century portraits of Native Americans and a Victorian chair that had been in the White House during the Lincoln administration. Mrs. Kennedy's White House tour is said to have been the first TV documentary special aimed at a female audience. But it wasn't just women watching. The show, which also aired on ABC the following evening, was seen by three out of four Americans with television sets.

She was home in bed at an early hour, and Jack finished the evening at a private party in the company of actress Angie Dickinson and his PT corps buddy Red Fay, soon to become an undersecretary of the Navy.

Jackie had decidedly mixed feelings about becoming a public figure, but she took the responsibility of being first lady very seriously. To her horror, she found that the White House had the ambience of a grand hotel that had been allowed to go to seed. The furniture was nondescript, and institutional drinking fountains lined the hallways. Relying on the advice of two socialite friends, Bunny Mellon and Jayne Wrightsman, Jackie moved astutely to create a Fine Arts Committee, responsible for raising private funds and overseeing the acquisition of appropriate period furniture. Henry du Pont, a multimillionaire expert on American furniture, was recruited as chairman. Jackie's preference for all things French sometimes clashed with the ideas of

du Pont, a champion of authentic Americana, and led to carping from Washington columnists. Still, the reaction to her restoration project was overwhelmingly favorable.

As a hostess, Jackie mixed high culture with café society sophistication. Intimate round tables replaced the traditional long banquet tables at state dinners. Chef René Verdon, formerly of Le Pavillon, took over the White House kitchen. Cocktails reappeared, as did cigarette smoking—banned by the Eisenhowers. At times, Jackie's tastes recalled the excesses attributed to Marie Antoinette at Versailles. At a private party for journalist Joseph Alsop during the early days of the administration, the centerpiece was a gold bucket filled with ten pounds of Sevruga caviar. The caviar was a gift, so the taxpayers were none the worse off. Still, it was difficult to imagine that any other first couple could have gotten away with such a display of conspicuous excess.

Jack Kennedy's own cultural tastes were more middle brow. He enjoyed the musical *Guys and Dolls* and the stand-up comedy of Bob Newhart. Reminiscing about his reaction to cellist Pablo Casals's being invited to play at a state dinner, Jack recalled, "I didn't know what the hell he played. Someone had to tell me." But he did believe that the White House should be a gathering place for highly accomplished people from across the political spectrum. Casals, known for his opposition to the Franco regime in Spain, played at the same November 1961 state dinner attended by aviators Charles and Anne Morrow Lindbergh, who had not visited the White House since their involvement with the anti-interventionist America First movement on the eve of World War II. Another state dinner, held in April 1962, would bring together American winners of the Nobel prize.

Opinion polls reflected the public's love affair with the new president. Pollster Lou Harris found that 73 percent of Americans had a favorable opinion of Kennedy, a higher rating than either FDR or Eisenhower had enjoyed during the early days of their first terms. White House secretaries were stunned by the volume and quality of the mail that poured in. The public asked the kind of questions that fans pose in letters to their favorite movie stars. People wanted to know, for example, whether Jackie wore hair rollers to bed, and if so, what the president had to say about it. Even the historian James MacGregor Burns, the author of a laudatory biography published before the election, was taken aback by the

The First Daughter
Jackie tried to protect her children's privacy, and Jack usually waited until she was away from the White House before allowing photographers to shoot candid pictures of Caroline and John Jr. Here, however, she posed reading aloud to Caroline.

CAROLINE AND JOHN JR.

A mischievous John-John entertains JFK's private secretary, Evelyn Lincoln.

A mong the most enduring images of the Kennedy White House were the photos taken of JFK working in the Oval Office while his young children played on the carpet. An adoring public learned that Caroline had a pony named Macaroni and thought affectionately of John Jr. as "John-John," a baby nickname that he would be saddled with for years. There hadn't been presidential children in the White House since the Theodore Roosevelt administration, and the presence of Caroline and John Jr. affirmed that, indeed, "the torch had been passed to a new generation," as John Kennedy predicted in his inaugural address.

adulation being heaped on Jack by an adoring press, and he wondered if the pro-Kennedy mood wasn't a little too euphoric to last. The prevailing verdict of the press, wrote Burns in *The New Republic*, was that Kennedy was "the handsomest, the best-dressed, the most articulate, and graceful as a gazelle."

While the new first lady was energetically upgrading the White House's social and cultural image, her husband faced an array of challenges, including a sluggish economy and growing tension over civil rights demonstrations in the South. But it was the international crises that posed the greatest dangers. Never had the Soviet Union been so menacing. British prime minister Harold Macmillan expressed a not uncommon opinion when he wrote that the Soviets "have a buoyant economy and will soon outmatch Capitalist society in the race for material wealth." The Soviets had also captured the initiative in science and technology. The launching of Sputnik, the first space satellite, in 1957, was followed in April 1961 by the announcement that cosmonaut Yuri Gagarin had become the first human to orbit the Earth. Most dismaying, Communist partisans were on the brink of seizing control of anti-colonial movements in Southeast Asia, Africa and Latin America.

During the campaign, Kennedy had taken an especially tough line on Cuba. While Nixon proposed quarantining the island, he had called for supporting efforts to overthrow Fidel Castro. "If you can't stand up to Castro, how can you hope to stand up to Khrushchev?" he asked. Within days of the election, the CIA's deputy director of planning, Richard Bissell, arrived in Florida to brief Kennedy on the agency's already existing plan to train Cuban exiles as a paramilitary force. The original goal, which called for infiltrating the exiles back into Cuba to lead a guerrilla resistance, had been upgraded to a full-scale amphibious invasion involving about 1,500 men. Once the invaders established a beachhead on the southern coast, Bissell predicted, the Cuban people would rise up in rebellion.

The notion that the Cubans needed only a little encouragement to get rid of Castro might have been plausible a year earlier. But since taking power in January 1959, Castro had moved rapidly to consolidate

his power. Moreover, the existence of the exiles' training camps in Florida, Nicaragua and Guatemala had become an open secret, and the CIA would be only minimally successful in keeping newspapers from reporting details of the invasion plan. Why, then, did Bissell or anyone else think the plan had a chance for success? The answer lay in the one aspect of operation that remained under deep cover. Mobsters Sam Giancana and Santos Trafficante, furious about the closure of lucrative Havana casinos, had approached the CIA with an offer to put out a contract for Castro's murder. If all went well, Cuba's Maximum Leader would die even as the exiles were coming ashore on the island's southern coast.

This part of the project was too explosive to commit to paper, and there remains no documentary proof that Kennedy gave his approval. However, Bissell later testified before Congress that he believed Kennedy had been briefed by then CIA chief Allen Dulles, and Thomas Powers, who wrote an authoritative book on the subject, concluded that Kennedy did indeed authorize Castro's assassination. This conclusion is bolstered by the fact that during this entire period Kennedy had his own back channel to Sam Giancana. In February 1960, Frank Sinatra had introduced him to Judith Campbell, later known as Judith Exner, the beautiful daughter of a well-to-do Los Angeles architect. Campbell became Jack's mistress and, as she later acknowledged, she also served as an intermediary between him and Giancana, another of her lovers.

During the early months of the Kennedy administration, pressure to go ahead with the Cuban invasion mounted. The exiles were clamoring for action, Castro's tiny air force was expecting reinforcements in the form of Soviet MIG fighters, and the president of Guatemala was pressing the CIA to shut down the training camp for the Cuban expeditionary force that had been established in his country.

Unfortunately, Kennedy's loosely structured staff was ill prepared to coordinate a project that involved the CIA, the Joint Chiefs of Staff, and—unofficially, of course—the mob. On March 15, for example, the landing site for the invasion was shifted from the city of Trinidad to the Bay of Pigs, 100 miles to the west.

Judith Campbell Exner
After her 1958 divorce from character actor Billy Campbell, Judy began dating Frank Sinatra, who introduced her to Jack Kennedy at the famed Sands Hotel in Las Vegas.

The Invasion?

In the confusion that followed the April 17, 1961 Bay of Pigs invasion, news organizations in both Cuba and America reported landings and naval engagements all around the island (as suggested by the numbers on this map from the time) that were mostly fictitious. In fact, the only troop landing took place at the Bay of Pigs (number 2 on the map).

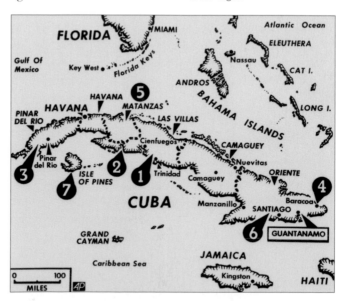

DEATH OF A WRITER

July 2, 1961
• Nobel and Pulitzer prize-winning novelist Ernest Hemingway died from a shotgun wound to the head. In the end, words failed the author of *The Sun Also Rises* and other classic books; he left no note to explain his apparent suicide.

The Bay of Pigs

Within hours of the first landings at the Bay of Pigs, the Cuban army had 50 antiaircraft guns in place. Pinned down on the beachheads, the anti-Castro Brigade was soon outnumbered two hundred to one.

As the plan inched forward, White House meetings tended to bog down into bull sessions on the morality of geopolitical power politics. Allen Dulles had warned that Castro was fast transforming Cuba into a Soviet client state. But Senator J. William Fulbright of Arkansas, invited by the president to sit in on an April 4 meeting, reflected the more romanticized view of Castro still prevalent in some quarters. Wasn't it possible, he wondered aloud, that Castro might yet succeed in "making Cuba a little paradise, a real pearl of the Antilles"? More substantially, Fulbright argued that unilateral military incursions were obsolete in the post–World War II era and a violation of existing treaties, including the 1948 charter of the Organization of American States.

Judging from his inaugural address, Kennedy had no doubts about the morality of fighting totalitarianism. Action against Cuba was also consistent with longstanding principles of American foreign policy, which held that no Old World power would be allowed to establish a military presence in the Western Hemisphere. Still, Kennedy was open to Fulbright's arguments. He had just launched the Alliance for Progress, a multi-year foreign aid plan intended to create more neighborly relations between the United States and Latin America, and he dreaded seeing the U.S. cast as an imperialist bully. Also, despite his repeated calls for Americans to display a spirit of sacrifice, he hadn't forgotten the message of *Why England Slept*: Citizens in a democracy have limited patience for military action unless they can see a direct threat to their national security. Kennedy didn't want to appear weak, but he also didn't want to use up the goodwill enjoyed by his young administration on a military adventure that might prove inconclusive, or worse.

THE PEACE CORPS

JFK signs the Peace Corps Act into law on September 22, 1961. Sargent Shriver, the Corps' first director, is at the far left. senator Hubert Humphrey, standing just to the right of the American flag, had been the first to propose the idea.

On March 1, 1961, President Kennedy signed an executive order establishing the Peace Corps. Sargent Shriver, the husband of the president's sister Eunice, was appointed as director. At first, the Peace Corps faced opposition from both Republicans and Democrats. Some condemned it as a publicity gimmick and a waste of taxpayer dollars, while others worried that it would backfire by exporting bohemian students to countries where they were bound to get into trouble. Congress didn't officially authorize the new agency until September.

In the meantime, Shriver's office had been swamped with letters asking for information; more than 5,000 applicants took the initial entry exams. At the end of August the first 51 volunteers arrived in Ghana, where they impressed government officials by singing the Ghanaian national anthem in Twi, the official language. By the end of 1963, 7,500 volunteers were at work in 44 countries. Over the years, the corps began accepting more mature recruits. One recent volunteer was 82. By 2002 more than 165,000 Americans had served in overseas assignments.

THE SINATRA CONNECTION

Frank Sinatra has Jack's ear at a fund-raising dinner. In addition to recording "High Hopes," the Kennedy campaign song, the crooner reportedly served as a conduit for substantial contributions from the Mob, delivering cash skimmed from Nevada casino operations to Joe Kennedy.

In 1959, Joe Kennedy invited Frank Sinatra to Hyannis Port, where he urged the singer to carry a message to Mafia kingpin Sam Giancana, asking him to use all the mob's resources to make sure that Jack prevailed in Illinois and West Virginia, a heavily unionized state. As Tina Sinatra later told Kennedy biographer Seymour Hersh, her father met Giancana on a golf course and put in a good word for Jack. JFK won both states, and in some quarters Giancana got credit for neutralizing union leaders who would have otherwise supported Nixon.

Jack socialized with Sinatra and his Rat Pack in Las Vegas during his presidential campaign, and in March 1962 he was expected to spend the weekend at Sinatra's home in Palm Springs. Sinatra remodeled his house,

even constructing a helipad in the expectation that Kennedy would be using Palm Springs as his West Coast retreat. But the FBI had been tapping some of Giancana's phone conversations, and Robert Kennedy was frantic with worry that the Sinatra connection was about to mushroom into a major scandal. Sinatra pal Peter Lawford, who was married to Jack's sister Patricia, was dispatched at the last minute to tell the crooner that the president would be staying with Bing Crosby instead. Sinatra was furious.

In the end, Kennedy gave a green light to the invasion, but with the proviso that the U.S. would be able to preserve what the CIA called "plausible deniability." No U.S. personnel would be directly—or at least visibly—involved. This limitation made an already unlikely plan virtually suicidal. But no one said this outright. CIA agents coordinating the project believed that Kennedy was just trying to preserve his personal deniability quotient and would not allow the operation to fail. Once the exiles had established a beachhead and could claim to represent an anti-Castro revolutionary government, he would call in air support.

At dawn on April 15, eight WWII-surplus B-26 bombers strafed Cuban airfields. An hour later, the pilot of another B-26 landed in Miami, claiming that the strikes were the work of himself and three other defecting Cuban air force pilots. Even as the American ambassador to the United Nations, Adlai Stevenson, was repeating this story in New York, reporters in Miami were dismissing it as a clumsy fabrication. The planes involved in the attack had actually taken off from Nicaragua and were flown by CIA-trained Cuban exiles. The B-26 that landed in Miami was just a decoy.

Needless to say, Fidel Castro was not dead. The Mafia's assassination plan fizzled when poison pills hidden inside a refrigerator froze to the coils and became unusable. Meanwhile, the president, in an excess of caution, had reduced the initial B-26 strike force from the original request for sixteen planes. On the recommendation of the State Department, he also canceled a second wave of attacks scheduled to coincide with the Monday morning troop landings. The stage was set for a military catastrophe. Castro's air force had not been wiped out by the B-26 raids. Enough planes survived to sink or run off the invaders' supply ships and keep their troops pinned down until they were surrounded. In keeping with Kennedy's decision not to involve American forces directly, the Oval Office refused Dick Bissell's pleas to launch planes from the aircraft carrier *Essex*, a few miles offshore. In the rout that followed, 114 men from the exile army were killed and 1,189 were taken prisoner. Cuban security forces also rounded up and jailed thousands of suspected sympathizers.

Kennedy called the Bay of Pigs debacle "the worst experience of my life." His self-confidence was badly shaken, his administration's aura of invincibility shattered. With hindsight, there would be plenty of blame to go around.

JEWISH JUSTICE

In December 1961, an Israeli court sentenced Nazi SS henchman Adolf Eichmann to death for "crimes against the Jewish people." Eichmann, who had been captured in Argentina, claimed he was only following orders.

Enemy Castro
After the Bay of Pigs, Jack and Bobby Kennedy were determined to eliminate the Cuban dictator, but through means that could never be traced directly to them.

AGENT 007

The 1962 film *Dr. No*, Sean Connery's debut as James Bond was screened repeatedly by JFK in the White House.

Kennedy gave the American career of James Bond an enormous boost in 1961 when he answered a query from *Life* magazine about his ten favorite books by listing Ian Fleming's *From Russia With Love* at number nine. Fleming had worked in British Naval intelligence during World War II, and the tuxedo-clad Bond, who preferred his martinis "shaken, not stirred," was a fantasy figure for many in the Kennedy administration. According to author Evan Thomas, Kennedy had played host to Fleming at a private dinner party in Georgetown before the election, where the British author entertained the guests by suggesting various ways to destabilize Castro's regime, including dropping dollar bills from airplanes and spreading the rumor that Castro was impotent. Whether Fleming realized it or not, his amusing ideas were similar in spirit to some of the proposals the CIA was actually considering, such as poisoning Castro with a toxic cigar.

There had been massive failures of intelligence, operational management, interagency communications and just plain common sense. Despite the president's stated desire to avoid direct U.S. involvement, or at least the appearance of it, American contract employees of the CIA were among the first to reach the beach, and two American destroyers were clearly visible from the Cuban shore. There was simply no chance that the role of the United States in the operation could be disguised. However, by insisting on "plausible deniability," Kennedy appeared to be conceding the argument that the operation was morally indefensible.

It would be unfair to hold Kennedy and his advisors entirely responsible for the underlying confusion of aims that led to the defeat. Their ambivalence reflected a deep division among American intellectuals over just when—or if—the use of force was justifiable in pursuit of winning the cold war. Unfortunately, the failures of April 1961 did not lead to greater clarity on this subject. The administration continued to rely heavily on covert operations, in part because they made it possible to avoid an open debate that would inevitably divide the Democratic Party and weaken the president politically. After the failed invasion, covert operations in Cuba continued. Bobby Kennedy, now one of the few advisors who had his brother's complete confidence, put heavy pressure on the CIA to bring about the assassination of Castro.

Ironically enough, Kennedy's popularity actually rose after the Bay of Pigs debacle. The American public liked his hard-line rhetoric and was prepared to rally around a leader at a time of military crisis, even if his plan had gone awry. According to a Gallup poll, 83 percent of Americans—10 percent more than before the Bay of Pigs—now had a favorable opinion of the president.

A Sobering Defeat

JFK was more accessible to the press than any previous occupant of the White House. Correspondents loved his graceful wit, but when Kennedy met the press after the Bay of Pigs debacle his mood was sober. As his friend Chuck Spalding put it, before that day Kennedy saw the presidency as a "glorious adventure." Afterward, he was haunted by the knowledge that others would pay with their lives for his mistakes.

A Leader
Challenged
1962

Two months after the Bay of Pigs invasion, the Kennedys departed on a mission to Europe that would restore some of the luster to their image. Jackie's chic appearance and knowledge of his country's language and culture impressed France's president, Gen. Charles de Gaulle, and delirious crowds cheered her every appearance. "I am the man who accompanied Jacqueline Kennedy to Paris," the president quipped, "and I have enjoyed it." Judging from the initial press coverage, the handsome first couple also scored a success at the scheduled summit meeting in Vienna. Photographed next to the dumpy, unappealing Khrushchevs, Jack and Jackie radiated health, vitality, and sophistication.

Behind the scenes, however, the talks did not go well for the Americans. Kennedy, engaging in his first summit, was all too conscious of the possibility that a misunderstood remark could have disastrous consequences. Khrushchev, a seasoned debater and expert bluffer, sized up his opposite number as inexperienced and indecisive. He shocked Kennedy by appearing unfazed by the possibility of all-out nuclear war. The experience persuaded the president that only a hard-line stance would work in dealing with the Soviets, whose strategy was to probe American policy for any sign of weakness and use the threat of a nuclear holocaust to get their way.

The main issue on Khrushchev's agenda at Vienna was the status of West Berlin, an island of capitalism completely surrounded by the territory of the Soviet-dominated German

KENNEDY AND KHRUSHCHEV

Khrushchev correctly sized up Kennedy as inexperienced and tried to bully him into making concessions.

Like Nixon, JFK had campaigned as a determined cold warrior. An early test of his resolve came in June 1961, when he met with Soviet premier Nikita Khrushchev at an informal summit meeting in Vienna. Press accounts at the time described the meeting as relatively "cordial" and focused on trivialities like Khrushchev's admiration for Jackie and her chic pink-beaded ball gown. ("I just love Russian dogs," the first lady told the Soviet leader.) Privately, Kennedy was stunned by Khrushchev's aggressive rhetoric. Khrushchev had threatened to start a nuclear war over control of Berlin, and when JFK commented that 70 million people might die in such a conflict, he shrugged off the warning as being of no importance.

Democratic Republic. East Germany was still a major economic power but shortages of consumer goods and limitations on personal freedom were causing a steady flow of refugees, mainly able-bodied workers, to flee to the free side of Berlin. Khrushchev threatened to sign a treaty with East Germany that would mandate cutting off West Germany's access to West Berlin.

Two months later, on August 13, Jack and Jackie were in Hyannis Port enjoying a Sunday afternoon sail when word came that East German troops had strung barbed wire barricades along the 27-mile border between the eastern and western sectors of Berlin. Within days, the wire would be replaced by a barrier of concrete blocks known to the East Germans as the "Democratic Protection Anti-Fascist Wall." The Kennedy administration took the position that the need to build a wall to keep one's own people in was an admission of weakness.

The people of West Berlin weren't so sure. Fearing that the wall was just a prelude to an effort to starve them into submission, 300,000 West Berliners took to the streets demanding American action. A telegram from Willy Brandt, the West Berlin mayor, warned that without some assurance of U.S. support, West Germans would begin to flee, turning his city into a "ghetto."

Kennedy responded by dispatching Vice President Johnson and Gen. Lucius Clay, the organizer of the 1948 Berlin airlift, to reassure the West Berliners. They arrived by plane, in time to greet the First Battle Group of the U.S. Army's 18th Infantry, which traveled via the Autobahn from West Germany. Despite tense confrontations with Soviet sentries, the Army convoy was allowed to pass. The principle of free access to West Berlin had been successfully tested.

Although West Berlin was theoretically the responsibility of World War II's Allied powers, in practice the crisis had devolved into a one-on-one confrontation between the U.S. and the Soviet Union. Kennedy regarded the wall as a defensive strategy and had no intention of going to war over it, but the anxieties of the West Berliners had persuaded him that it was necessary to take a firm stand against Soviet encroachment. With Gen. Clay choreographing an intricate series of symbolic but provocative gestures, Great Britain and France had opted to remain in the background. The British contributed just

three armored personnel vehicles to the Autobahn convoy and the French none at all. Lyndon Johnson, on his return to Washington, stressed the "fantastic dependence" that the Free World had placed on America. Whether this dependence was entirely voluntary or not, he was essentially correct. In the nuclear age, frictions that once might have developed over a period of months could reach a critical stage within a matter of days. And no one could predict where the next flashpoint would be.

Jack Kennedy's tumultuous first year in office ended with a family tragedy. On December 19, while golfing in Palm Beach, his 73-year-old father suffered a massive stroke. Joe's mind remained relatively alert, but he was paralyzed on one side and could communicate only through monosyllabic grunts and hand gestures. The man who had always told his children "Kennedys don't cry" was now frequently reduced to tears of frustration.

Joe's care was organized by his devoted niece, Ann Gargan. He saw little of Rose, becoming agitated and angry whenever she entered his room, and she reacted by delving deeper into her own private world. Always thrifty to a fault, Rose limited the hired help to one cup of coffee a day, while she sneaked onto the golf course to avoid paying greens fees and called on her son the president for advice about getting the aging washing machine repaired.

Jack's own health remained a touchy subject. Adm. George C. Burkley, a Navy physician, had joined his medical team after the inauguration, and Burkley soon became concerned about Dr. Janet Travell's reliance on daily procaine injections. Travell retained the title of White House physician but was eased into retirement. The president, meanwhile, initially resisted Burkley's recommendation of daily physical therapy on the grounds that the press would find out and begin to question his fitness.

Burkley didn't know it, but both Jack and Jackie continued to rely on the secret ministrations of Dr. Jacobson. Unable to get along without Jacobson's "vitamin" shots, Jack had even arranged for Jacobson to accompany him to the Vienna summit, traveling separately on a commercial airliner. By the summer of 1962, Bobby was so alarmed by his brother's growing dependence that he

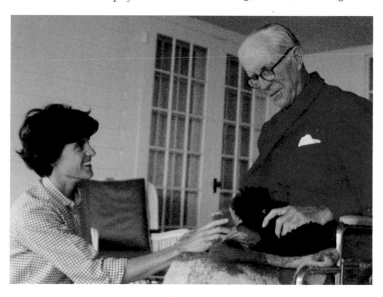

submitted samples of Jacobson's elixirs to the FDA, which reported the presence of amphetamines. Jack shrugged off Bobby's warnings.

Oddly enough, considering his worries that the press would make an issue of his health problems, Kennedy seemed to have no such fears about his extramarital affairs. As early as 1958, a morally outraged woman named

PEACE BY PICASSO

April 30, 1962
• The Soviet Union awarded artist Pablo Picasso the Lenin Peace Prize. The socialist painter's image of a dove of peace had become a symbol of communism, although most of his work was banned in the Soviet Union.

Silenced Patriarch

Jack had often been at odds with his father, but Joe's stroke in December 1961 deprived him of the advice of a man who never feared being thought cynical or politically incorrect. Largely unable to communicate after the stroke, Joe relied on the companionship of his devoted niece, Ann Gargan, the daughter of Rose's sister Agnes.

Florence Kater had launched a campaign to expose Jack's dalliance with his aide Pamela Turnure, who rented the upper floor of Kater's Georgetown home. Kater wrote letters to dozens of newspaper editors and even picketed the White House. The press ignored her, and so did Jack Kennedy, who entertained women too numerous to count in the White House while the first lady retreated to Glen Ora, the Kennedys' rented estate in the Virginia hunt country.

The elaborate arrangements for sneaking women into the White House involved deliverymen, West Wing typists, and high-level officials. Others around the president, including some members of his Secret Service detail, were inspired to follow his example and engage in hard partying. Rumors flew around Washington that certain diplomats and lobbyists had brought attractive females to town in the hope that they would catch the president's eye. The situation made the administration ripe for blackmail and scandal.

The FBI had known about Sam Giancana's overtures to the CIA since October 1960. By February 1962 the bureau's investigation of Giancana and his associate Johnny Roselli had led them to Judith Campbell, whose phone records showed dozens of person-to-person calls placed to Kennedy's personal secretary, Evelyn Lincoln. (Jack once said of Lincoln that if he told her he had cut off Jackie's head, she would immediately run to fetch him a hatbox.) On March 22, J. Edgar Hoover met with the president to report the FBI's findings and warn him against further contacts with Campbell. Outraged, Kennedy interpreted the meeting as a power play on Hoover's part. He stopped socializing with Frank Sinatra, the man who had introduced him to Campbell, but his calls to her continued.

In August, FBI agents watching Campbell's apartment happened to observe a break-in conducted by two men who were found to be the sons of a security officer employed by the General Dynamics corporation. The implication was that they were planting a listening device in the hope of getting information that could provide leverage for the company, which was in the process of bidding for a major defense contract.

Kennedy did not begin to appreciate the risks he was taking until June 1963 when the Profumo scandal broke in Great Britain. Much like Jack Kennedy, John Profumo, the British minister of war, was a World War II hero with a beautiful wife and a great favorite of reporters, who admired his wit and sophistication. But the press turned on Profumo with a vengeance when he was caught cavorting with a ring of party girls who may or may not have been passing on his pillow talk to a Soviet military attaché. Kennedy pumped his journalist friend Ben Bradlee for the latest inside information on Profumo, and with good reason. He'd dated at least two of the girls involved in the scandal during their visits to New York and been seen with one of them, Suzy Chang, lunching at the 21 Club.

Shady Figure

The Chicago mob boss was overheard on an FBI wiretap boasting that he was responsible for getting Jack Kennedy elected. Giancana was bitter when FBI surveillance of him and his associates continued, even as he was working with the CIA to assassinate Castro. Giancana was murdered in 1975.

1962, A YEAR OF TRIUMPH AND TURMOIL

The president and John Glenn inspect the *Friendship 7* space capsule that had recently carried Glenn into orbit. Kennedy had made the race to the moon a top priority of his administration.

The year 1962 began with a dramatic demonstration of American prowess in science and technology. Lt. Col. John H. Glenn, Jr., became the first American to orbit the Earth, completing three circuits in four hours and 55 minutes. The year also saw the first transatlantic television broadcast (via a Telstar communications satellite) and the introduction of the industrial robot. American scientist James D. Watson shared the Nobel prize with Britain's Francis Crick and Maurice Wilkins for their discovery of the structure of DNA. "Moon River" was the year's Grammy-winning song, and a young comedian named Johnny Carson became host of the *Tonight* show.

But underneath the prevailing mood of optimism and social tranquility, there were disturbing hints of the years of turmoil to come. While the president was preoccupied with the Cuban missile crisis, which had brought the superpowers to the brink of war, Martin Luther King Jr. was leading civil rights marches in Georgia, and the campus of Harvard University was in the grip of an LSD craze. For an increasing number of college students, the romantic sound of Henry Mancini was passé. They were listening to Bob Dylan's gravel-voiced anthem "Blowin' in the Wind."

MARY PINCHOT MEYER

Of many many women who had liaisons with President Kennedy, few were as enigmatic as Mary Pinchot Meyer. The ex-wife of CIA deputy director Cord Meyer and sister-in-law of *Washington Post* editor Ben Bradlee, Mary Meyer was part of a circle of Georgetown socialites who obtained LSD from Timothy Leary in 1962. While there is no evidence that Meyer used LSD with the president as Leary later suggested, it is entirely possible. LSD was being touted in those days as a miracle drug that elevated its users to a higher level of consciousness, and numerous highly placed

Jack with Mary Pinchot Meyer, far right, and her sister, Tony Bradlee. Their mother, Ruth Pinchot, in dark glasses, was an ardent Goldwater supporter.

individuals had tried it out of curiosity, including *Time* and *Life* publisher Henry Luce and various CIA officers.

Leary later suggested that Meyer's murder in 1964 was part of some obscure CIA plot, but the evidence supports the prosecutors' contention that Mary Meyer was shot in a mugging gone awry. At any rate Ray Crump, Jr., the man arrested for the killing, was ultimately acquitted.

By late summer, Kennedy was threatened by a Profumo-style scandal of his own. The Senate Rules committee was investigating Bobby Baker, the secretary to the Democratic Party members of the Senate, and a well-known Capitol Hill fixer. Baker had introduced Jack Kennedy to Ellen Rometsch, a Liz Taylor look-alike suspected by many of being an East German spy. On August 21, 1963, just days after the FBI opened a counterintelligence file on Rometsch, the State Department abruptly ordered her deportation. Traveling on a U.S. Air Force transport plane, Rometsch departed for Germany, where she would be beyond the reach of Senate investigators.

The Bay of Pigs had revealed the limitations of inspired amateurism as an approach to foreign affairs. Kennedy's efforts to forge a constructive policy on Southeast Asia demonstrated that the president of the United States, for all his apparent power, was often forced to choose among decidedly unappealing options. Kennedy considered the region too important to cede to the

Communists, but perhaps not quite important enough to justify a major ground war fought by American troops.

The U.S. had endorsed a neutral regime in Laos. But North Vietnamese troops continued to support Communist insurgents, and Kennedy soon countered by authorizing the CIA to conduct its own covert operations. In South Vietnam, the administration hoped to achieve its aims by supporting the government of President Ngo Dinh Diem, a devout Roman Catholic. By the end of 1962, some 11,000 military "advisors" had been dispatched, ostensibly to train South Vietnamese troops and assist the Diem regime in implementing the strategic hamlets program, which aimed to create fortified villages immune to Viet Cong penetration. Unfortunately Diem often seemed more interested in persecuting Buddhists than defeating Communists, and his government's heavy-handed implementation of the program alienated the very peasants it was supposed to win over. As the year ended, the administration seemed to be drifting into a deeper involvement without a clear plan for a military victory.

In his memoirs, Richard Nixon recalled a conversation he had with Kennedy around the time of the Bay of Pigs. "It really is true that foreign affairs is the only important issue for a president to handle, isn't it?" Kennedy said. "I mean, who gives a shit if the minimum wage is $1.15 or $1.25 in comparison to something like this?" In fact, Kennedy did worry about fighting inflation and spurring economic growth, but he never managed to develop a coherent economic policy, and his confrontational style made the business community nervous. When the major steel companies raised their prices shortly after signing new labor agreements that included wage concessions, Kennedy took the increases as a personal affront and publicly

Conflict in Vietnam

As efforts to work in partnership with President Diem faltered, U.S. military advisors were being drawn into combat against the Viet Cong. In private, Kennedy expressed dismay over the escalating conflict, but he publicly affirmed his resolve to carry on.

threatened reprisals. His stern words played well with the public, but the press and economists were critical. Columnist David Lawrence, in a typical response, accused the president of practicing "quasi-fascism." Not surprisingly, the stock market swooned. The Dow Jones average, which had hovered around 690 before the confrontation began, fell from 611 to 563 in a single day, an event variously labeled "Blue Monday" or "the Kennedy crash."

One domestic issue the president was forced to confront was civil rights. During the 1960 campaign, Kennedy impressed black voters when he made a personal phone call to Coretta Scott King after her husband was ordered to serve four months in a Georgia jail. His call raised expectations that his administration would act as a vigorous advocate for the civil rights movement. Nothing of the kind happened. When it came to social issues, Kennedy's instincts were invariably cautious. Once in office, he took steps to revise federal policies that contributed to discrimination, but he had serious qualms about groups like the Freedom Riders who were traveling throughout the South, integrating bus depots and lunch counters. He resisted calls to punish the entire South by cutting off federal aid, and he hesitated to call out the Army to quell disturbances, creating the impression that the South was occupied territory as it had been in the aftermath of the Civil War.

A cynical view of Kennedy's position was that he feared alienating Southern Democrats, whose support he needed to get reelected and pass key legislation on Medicare, international trade, and other issues. But Ted Sorenson, in his account of the Kennedy years, emphasized his boss's concern for preserving "the fabric of our social order—to prevent the unsatisfied grievances of an entire race from rending that fabric in two." In fact, the growing militancy of the civil rights movement had put the federal government in a reactive position, the sort of situation that Kennedy always found uncomfortable.

In September 1962, the Fifth Circuit of the U.S. Court of Appeals ordered the University of Mississippi to admit a black student, James Meredith. Gov. Ross Barnett was willing to enroll Meredith, but only if federal marshals ordered him to do so at gunpoint. Unwilling to stage such a melodramatic photo opportunity, Kennedy balked.

Negotiations with Barnett broke down, and news that Meredith had arrived at the university's Oxford campus touched off a riot. Frantic that Meredith would be killed, Kennedy now had no choice but to call out the Army, but the troops did not arrive in time to quell the violence. A French reporter and a local bystander were killed. In the end, 23,000 soldiers were deployed to get Meredith safely to his first class.

The Oxford riot severely tested Jack's nerves. At the height of the confusion, he summoned Dr. Jacobson from New York to administer instant confidence in the form of one of his miraculous shots. Afterward, both the president and his brother Bobby were irate about the Army's slow deployment and critical of their own

Meredith VS. Mississippi

Meredith's legal battle for the right to register at the all-white Oxford campus of the University of Mississippi ended when Supreme Court justice Hugo Black, an Alabaman, intervened in his favor. Lengthy mediation by the White House failed to prevent a riot, and Kennedy sent federal troops to end the violence.

inability to work out a peaceful solution. But once again, to Kennedy's amazement, public opinion supported him. Most Americans were satisfied that he had shown an appropriate combination of restraint and toughness.

Even as the situation in Oxford was developing, the White House was learning that U-2 spy planes had observed Soviet construction teams building surface-to-air missile launching sites in Cuba. Within a few weeks, new information gave the lie to the Soviet claim that it was providing the Cubans with defensive weapons only. American intelligence estimated that there were 10,000 Soviet troops on the island—actually, there were four times that many—along with fighter jets and other advanced weapons. At least six medium-range nuclear missile sites were under construction, along with three sites for launching longer-range missiles, capable of reaching all but a tiny corner of the continental U.S.

The president appointed a high-level advisory panel, known as ExCom, to suggest options. One obvious possibility was an immediate surgical strike to knock out the missile sites. Bobby Kennedy immediately objected, calling the plan "Pearl Harbor in reverse" and declaring that he didn't want his brother Jack to be "the Tojo of the 1960s." Former secretary of state Dean Acheson, who had been invited to sit in on the panel as an elder statesman, found this remark typical of the attorney general's sincere but essentially immature brand of idealism. In the end ExCom voted against an invasion, in part because it could not be sure that the Cubans lacked the capacity to retaliate with a nuclear attack against U.S. territory.

On Monday, October 22, Kennedy gave a radio address announcing that the U.S. had thrown up a naval quarantine around Cuba. If Khrushchev chose to defy the quarantine, the almost inevitable result would be nuclear war. The president's announcement won overwhelming support from Americans. Moreover, faced with the destabilizing and frightening presence of Soviet missiles in Cuba, the

Crisis in Cuba

While awaiting the Soviet response to the naval blockade of Cuba, the president conferred regularly with an ad hoc group of high-level advisors known as ExCom, short for Executive Committee of the National Security Council. To avoid the kind of miscommunications that occurred during the Bay of Pigs invasion, ExCom held lengthy deliberations.

A TELSTAR IS BORN

The Telstar satellite beamed the first live TV transmission across the Atlantic on July 11, 1962, when Americans watched French movie star Yves Montand perform a song in "real time."

MARILYN MONROE

In May 1962, television viewers who tuned in to see President Kennedy's gala 45th birthday party and fundraiser, broadcast from Madison Square Garden in New York, were amazed to see Marilyn Monroe, in a skintight flesh-colored gown, waddle to the podium to deliver a breathy, seductive rendition of "Happy Birthday, Mr. President." Kennedy made a joke of the incident, saying, "I can now retire from politics after hearing 'Happy Birthday' sung to me in such a sweet, wholesome way."

The evening's emcee, Peter Lawford, and other Kennedy intimates were well aware that Jack Kennedy and Marilyn had been having a sporadic affair since the

Introduced as "the late Marilyn Monroe," the notoriously unpunctual sex goddess caused a sensation with her appearance at the Madison Square Garden birthday gala. She never saw Jack Kennedy again.

previous November, and doubtless they admired him for it. But they had made a serious error in allowing Monroe to flaunt the relationship in public. A troubled woman, increasingly dependent on alcohol and drugs, Monroe had begun to imagine that Jack Kennedy was in love with her. After the gala, Kennedy refused to take Monroe's calls, and the task of placating her fell to his brother Bobby. Less than three months later, Monroe was dead from an apparent overdose of sleeping pills.

Organization of American States voted unanimously to back the blockade. In Europe, even the usually critical Charles de Gaulle agreed to support the American position, in the face of a hostile French press.

Still, two days later Kennedy and his aides were on the verge of despair as they followed reports that two Soviet ships with a submarine escort were approaching the blockade line. At the last minute, the ships stopped dead in the water. "We're eyeball to eyeball, and I think the other guy just blinked," said Secretary of State Dean Rusk.

In truth, before the crisis was over, both sides would blink more than once. Aware of the need to let Khrushchev save face, Kennedy decided to let a Soviet oil tanker pass through the blockade line. And when a U-2 surveillance plane was shot down over Cuba by a SAM missile, he decided not to retaliate. The blockade ended after 13 days with a negotiated solution. Khrushchev agreed to dismantle Soviet missile sites in Cuba, over the

objections of Castro. In return, American-made missiles were removed from bases in Turkey and other sites close to the border of the Soviet Union, and the U.S. promised not to invade Cuba in the future.

The terms of the settlement were arguably the best that could be hoped for. While the loss of the Jupiters was a blow to Turkish pride, they were already considered technologically obsolete and the U.S. would soon replace them with submarine-based Polaris missiles. Contrary to the fears of some of Kennedy's advisors, the NATO alliance did not disintegrate. Khrushchev was one of history's great bluffers and, with hindsight, the U.S. was fortunate to have a president who had the nerve to call his bluff when it really mattered.

On the other hand, Kennedy's reluctance to report bad news created confusion about the aims of American policy, and his personal style generated unrealistic expectations. In December 1962, the administration struck a deal to exchange more than $53 million worth of pharmaceuticals, bulldozers, and other goods for the freedom of the imprisoned Cuban freedom fighters. That same month, the president and first lady appeared at a rally of Cuban Brigade supporters in Miami's Orange Bowl. Kennedy had expected a cool reception, and he had prepared a sober speech that reflected his two-month-old agreement with Khrushchev. But the 40,000 spectators greeted him with wild applause, and one of the released prisoners handed him a battle flag that he had managed to hide throughout a year and a half in captivity. Carried away by the emotion of the moment, Kennedy promised the crowd, "I can assure you that his flag will be returned to the brigade on Cuban soil."

The Prisoner's Return
Speaking in Spanish, the first lady addresses members of the Cuban Brigade 2506, whose release from Cuban prisons had been negotiated by the administration. The Kennedys had been warned that the crowd at the Orange Bowl rally might boo them, but they were greeted with loud cheers and applause.

Rendezvous
with Death
1963

Nineteen-sixty-three was shaping up to be a good year for the Kennedy presidency. On May 29, Jack celebrated his 46th birthday with a party aboard the presidential yacht *Sequoia*, dancing to the music of Chubby Checker's 1960 hit, "The Twist." As often happened when the Kennedy clan got together, the party had its rowdy moments. An inebriated guest stumbled into an antique engraving that had been Jackie's gift to her husband, poking a hole in it with his foot. Unflappable as usual, Jackie pretended not to mind.

In June, the president visited Berlin, where 150,000 onlookers cheered his passionate denunciation of the Berlin Wall. A month later, Secretary of State Dean Rusk joined a team of American negotiators in Moscow, where a chastened and much friendlier Premier Khrushchev agreed to a nuclear test ban treaty.

On August 7, while Jack was being briefed on the new treaty in the White House, he learned that his wife, vacationing on Cape Cod, had gone into premature labor. Patrick Bouvier Kennedy was born with hyaline membrane disease and lived only two days. Jackie was so depressed about losing the baby that her sister Lee suggested that Jackie and some friends join her and her current lover, Aristotle Onassis, who were cruising the Mediterranean on the Onassis yacht. Although photos of the first lady, strolling side by side with the flamboyant shipping magnate during a port call in Smyrna, would inspire some gossip, baby Patrick's death

had brought the first couple closer together. Jackie spent much of her time aboard Ari's yacht writing love letters to her husband. "I loved you from the first time I saw you," she said in one of them. "I'll show you how much I love you when I get back."

Civil rights remained a difficult issue for Jack Kennedy. Polls showed that a growing number of working-class whites believed that the federal authorities were moving too fast, trying to impose social changes that ought to come about gradually. Frustrated blacks, on the other hand, felt that the president still did not grasp the moral urgency of their demands. Even so, that summer there was reason for optimism. The administration had sent a civil rights bill to Congress that called for the desegregation of public facilities, and the White House had worked productively with the organizers of the March on Washington, which had proved to be a great success.

The CIA's covert operations in Cuba, shut down after the missile crisis, had been quietly reopened. Fidel Castro might still be in power, but the Cuban economy was in decline and Kennedy believed that the rest of Latin America no longer looked to Castro's regime as a model.

On October 26, Clark Mollenhoff reported in the *Des Moines Register* that the Senate Rules Committee still intended to investigate breaches of national security in connection with Ellen Rometsch's contacts with "several high executive branch officials." Two days later, the attorney general arranged for Senate Majority Leader Mike Mansfield and Senator Everett Dirksen, the minority leader, to meet with J. Edgar Hoover for a personal briefing. During the course of the meeting, Hoover casually revealed details of the amorous escapades of several senators from both parties. Enthusiasm for a public airing of the allegations about Ellen Rometsch was snuffed out in an instant.

On November 2, South Vietnamese president Ngo Dinh Diem and his brother Ngo Dinh Nhu were killed during the course of a successful military coup. The administration's role in these events remains a subject of debate. Certainly, one faction among Kennedy's advisors had concluded that Diem was a liability and rather clumsily signaled their readiness to support a change of regimes. According to biographer Herbert Parmet, Kennedy knew a coup was imminent and he had hoped to save Diem's life, dispatching his former Harvard roommate Torbert Macdonald on a confidential mission to warn Diem and urge him to seek asylum in the American embassy. But Diem had insisted on staying put. Kennedy was depressed by the murders, but many around

Onassis On Board

Jackie's decision to cruise the Mediterranean on Aristotle Onassis's yacht in a party that included her sister, Lee, and Franklin Roosevelt Jr. provoked criticism from the press and a slew of outraged letters. Many Americans were shocked that Mrs. Kennedy would associate with as disreputable a character as Onassis.

THE MARCH ON WASHINGTON

On August 28, 1963, some 200,000 demonstrators—about a quarter of them white—converged on Washington, answering the call for a massive "March on Washington for Jobs and Freedom." Kennedy's attitude toward the push for progress on civil rights had initially been cautious, and his Justice Department continued to monitor the movement nervously for signs that it was taking a radical direction. By the summer of 1963, however, Kennedy's attitude had changed. On June 11, he announced his intention to propose a comprehensive civil rights bill, and in July he gave his endorsement to the march.

The mood of the march was predominantly one of celebration, and Martin Luther King Jr.'s "I Have a Dream" speech was greeted with euphoric applause.

Organizers of the March on Washington met with President Kennedy later that day. Among those present, starting fourth from left, were Whitney Young, Martin Luther King Jr., John Lewis of the Student Non-Violent Coordinating Committee, Rabbi Joachim Prinz of the American Jewish Congress, Eugene P. Donnaly of the National Council of Churches, and labor leader A. Philip Randolph. To the right of the president are Vice President Johnson, labor leader Walter Reuther, and NAACP president Roy Wilkins.

After the rally at the Lincoln Memorial, King and other march leaders went directly to the White House, where Kennedy congratulated them on their success, posed for photographs, and ordered up an impromptu lunch from the kitchen. In a televised interview that evening, King called the day a milestone in "a revolution of rising expectations."

END OF ALCATRAZ

March 21, 1963
• The last 27 prisoners were removed from Alcatraz prison in the San Francisco Bay. The island penitentiary that once housed Al Capone had become too expensive to maintain.

A Quick Trip to Texas

On November 21, 1963, the Kennedys headed to Texas for a whirlwind tour, intended to rally Texas Democrats and inspire donations to the president's reelection campaign. Jack spoke at Brooks Air Force Base in San Antonio, the League of United Latin American Citizens in Austin, and, the following morning, to the Fort Worth Chamber of Commerce. Dallas was to be the next stop on the itinerary.

him believed that the developments in Saigon, however regrettable, would make a victory over the Viet Cong possible at last.

Kennedy would be up for reelection in 1964, and as the year drew to a close he had scheduled a number of political trips. He was not enthusiastic about his visit to Texas in late November. The state's Democrats were feuding, split between followers of Gov. John Connally and liberal Sen. Ralph Yarborough, and Dallas in particular was known to be a tough town for visiting politicians. The city was home base for a number of extremist groups that ran the gamut from black militants to the right-wing followers of Gen. Edwin A. Walker. Visiting the city a few weeks earlier, Adlai Stevenson had been confronted by a small but agitated group of demonstrators, including one woman who had conked him on the head with a picket sign.

But Texas was also home to a number of Democratic contributors with deep pockets. Moreover, Kennedy hoped to use his speech at the Dallas Trade Mart on Nov. 22 to reiterate his intention to stand fast against communist insurgencies around the world. "Our assistance to these nations can be painful, risky and costly, as is true in Southeast Asia today," said the text of his prepared speech for the occasion. "But we dare not weary of the task."

Despite an earlier announcement that Jackie's recuperation from childbirth would force her to cancel public engagements through the end of the year, she decided to accompany Jack to Texas. After stops in San Antonio, Houston, and Fort Worth, the presidential party arrived at Dallas's Love Field at 11:20 AM on the 22nd, just in time for the motorcade to the Trade Mart. A knot of hostile pickets greeted them, including one man with a sign that read YOU ARE A TRAITER (*sic*). A black-bordered advertisement in the day's edition of the *Dallas Morning News*, paid for by a group that called itself the American Fact-Finding Committee, accused Kennedy of losing Cuba and exchanging the Monroe Doctrine for "the Spirit of Moscow," a reference to the test ban treaty. But despite these signs of hostility, the Dallas crowds were overwhelmingly enthusiastic.

By 12:30, the motorcade had made its way through the downtown business district and reached Dealey Plaza. Just ahead lay the on-ramp to the Stemmons Freeway, which would carry the visiting dignitaries to the Trade Mart, where the city's most prominent Democrats were waiting to sit down to a roast beef luncheon. As the president's Lincoln convertible approached the underpass just before the freeway

entrance, Gov. Connally, seated in the jump seat in front of Jack Kennedy, looked over his shoulder and commented, "Mr. President, you can't say Dallas doesn't love you!"

Suddenly, there were two loud reports. Bill Greer, the driver of the presidential car, instinctively slowed, trying to locate the source of the noise. For an instant, the other passengers in the car failed to notice that a 6.5 mm bullet had passed through Jack Kennedy's neck. Exiting the president's throat, the bullet struck Connally in the back, passed through his chest and hit his right wrist and thigh. For an instant, Connally didn't realize that he had been shot. Then he felt a sharp pain in his back and realized that blood was pouring into his lap.

Jackie hadn't taken any particular notice of the reports. There was always a lot of noise when you were in a motorcade, motorcycles backfiring and so on. She was looking to her left, waving to the crowd, when she heard Connally cry out. Turning toward Jack, she saw that his hand was at his throat and he had what she later called "this sort of quizzical look on his face." Before she could react, another bullet slammed into her husband's head. His skull exploded, sending bone and brain matter flying.

In the months to come, she would replay those few seconds hundreds of times in her mind. If only she had been watching her husband, she would have seen the first bullet hit and pulled him down into her lap, perhaps saving his life.

A Dallas Welcome

It was good political theater for the president to disembark from *Air Force One* to the cheers of an enthusiastic crowd, so JFK's party made a 13-minute flight from Fort Worth to Dallas's Love Field.

THE ZAPRUDER FILM

The assassination of Kennedy was the work of seconds, but debate over exactly how it happened would go on for decades. Of all the spectators in Dealey Plaza on November 22, 1963, only Dallas dress manufacturer Abraham Zapruder managed to capture the entire sequence of events with his brand-new Bell & Howell Zoomatic camera. Later that day, Zapruder received a visit from a Secret Service agent. He agreed to have the 8mm film developed at once, and provided copies to the Secret Service. He then sold the original to *Life* magazine, whose editors agreed that the public should be spared seeing the more violent frames of film.

Over the years, while rights to the footage were controlled by *Life* and then the Zapruder family, many

Few images have captivated the world like the stark frames of the Zapruder film. In the top frame, President Kennedy and Texas Governor John Connally are wounded by what investigators later concluded was a single bullet. Moments later, in the bottom frame, Kennedy receives the second and fatal bullet to his head.

copies were made. In 1991 the *Today* show featured a version of the film that included a soundtrack with four clearly audible shots. But Zapruder's home movie was silent. If there were actually three shots, as most witnesses thought, and the second and third shots hit the president—not first and third, as hypothesized by most investigators—then there was ample time for a single assassin to have acted alone and most conspiracy theories about the assassination become moot.

A Shocked Nation

That weekend, stunned Americans devoured newspaper accounts of the assassination. Early stories were filled with misinformation. It was reported, for example, that the president had been struck first by a bullet that passed through his throat from front to back.

After Jack was shot for the second time, Jackie started to climb out onto the trunk of the Lincoln. Film of the assassination captured by a home movie enthusiast shows her leaning over the trunk, reaching out her hand. It is impossible to tell exactly what she was reaching for. Was she trying to help Secret Service man Clint Hill, who had leapt onto the back of the vehicle just as the driver stepped on the gas? Comedian Lenny Bruce did a riff on the subject, mocking the media for being too reverential to say what seemed obvious to Bruce himself: The first lady was trying to flee the scene and save her own life. Jackie herself would tell investigators that she had no memory of the incident. Much later, however, she would recall that she had instinctively tried to retrieve a piece of Jack's skull.

And, in fact, when the Lincoln reached Parkland Hospital four miles away, the first lady was clutching a piece of her husband's brain in one hand. Looking dazed, she handed it to Dr. Pepper Jenkins, an anesthesiologist who was among the first to respond to the emergency room page.

Adm. George Burkley, who had been riding in one of the cars behind the presidential limousine, reached Parkland seconds later. Whenever Kennedy traveled on official business, Burkley was unobtrusively in the background, ready to make sure that the president got the medications needed to increase an Addison's patient's chances of surviving an emergency surgical procedure. Burkley gave the trauma team some Solu-Cortef, a cortisone-based steroid, to add to the president's IV. But he knew the drug was useless. Kennedy's pupils

WHO WAS LEE HARVEY OSWALD?

After fatally shooting patrolman J. D. Tippit, Oswald ducked into a nearby movie theater. Cornered inside, Oswald was hustled to a police car by uniformed and plainclothes detectives.

Born in 1939, Lee Harvey Oswald had a troubled childhood. By the age of sixteen he had developed into an odd, belligerent youth who typically dealt with his frustrations by hitting his mother. Through solitary reading, young Oswald concluded that communism was the best system of government in the world and the solution to all his problems. After serving in the U.S. Marines in Japan, Oswald defected to the Soviet Union in 1959, but found that the Soviets—like his Marine superiors—failed to appreciate his talents. Two years later he returned to the U.S. with his Russian wife. His hero was now Fidel Castro, and he hoped to find some way to attract Castro's attention.

In September 1963, Castro gave an interview to the Associated Press, denouncing President Kennedy as a "cretin" and warning that if the U.S. took part in plots to kill Cuban leaders, "they themselves will not be safe." Reading these words in the newspapers, Oswald may have felt that the Maximum Leader was outlining a mission for him personally. Before he was killed by Dallas nightclub owner Jack Ruby, Oswald told police that he wanted to be represented by John Abt, an attorney best known for representing Gus Hall, chairman of the Communist Party USA.

were already fixed and dilated, his pulse indiscernible. Once the neurosurgeon on duty examined the massive wound at the rear of the patient's head, all attempts to revive him ceased.

News of John F. Kennedy's death spread quickly around the world. In London, the House of Commons adjourned out of respect. In Berlin, Mayor Willy Brandt's call to burn candles in the American president's memory gave rise to a spontaneous torchlight parade. In many nations, heads of state went on TV and the radio to deliver impromptu eulogies. Even Radio Moscow played solemn music. For Americans, the events of the day would take on special and terrible intimacy. The press buses that had been following the

A Grave in Arlington

Back at the White House on the morning after the assassination, the still dazed widow was asked to choose a site for her husband's grave. Overruling the Kennedy sisters, who assumed that Jack would be buried in the family plot in Brookline, Massachusetts, Jackie opted for Arlington National Cemetery. The site would become the most important memorial to JFK, drawing millions of visitors every year.

"I have a rendezvous with death At some disputed barricade"

FROM ALAN SEEGER'S "RENDEZVOUS WITH DEATH"

presidential motorcade arrived at Parkland Hospital within minutes of the lead car, and the aftermath of the assassination became the first national tragedy to be played out in real time on national television. Millions of Americans learned that the president had been shot when CBS anchorman Walter Cronkite broke into the afternoon's broadcast of the soap opera *As the World Turns*. By the time the death was officially announced an hour later, unconfirmed reports were already being aired, based on the overheard comment of a priest who had been called in to administer last rites. Scarcely another hour had passed before WFAA-TV cameraman Ron Reiland delivered his eyewitness account of the capture of the assassin, Lee Harvey Oswald.

Like so many others, Rose Kennedy heard about the shooting in Dallas from the television. Pacing compulsively, as she always did when troubled, Rose began to consider how to break the news to her husband. Joe had always said that the morning was the proper time to hear bad news, so she decided to wait until Saturday morning. But watching TV, especially the news, was one of Joe's few remaining pleasures. His nurse, a woman coincidentally named Rita Dallas, turned off the set in his room and told Joe that it was broken. His eyes telegraphed his disbelief. Later that afternoon, Ted arrived, followed by Eunice, both telling their father that they had just impulsively decided to pay a visit. Hoping to make the story about the broken television less of a transparent lie, Ted reached in the back of the set and pulled out a few wires. By the time Joe was informed of his son's death the following day, he obviously knew that something was terribly wrong. He wept unashamedly, but indicated that he wanted to know all the details. The family hastily summoned a TV repairman.

Two days later, on Sunday, an estimated 95 percent of American adults gathered in front of their television sets to watch the solemn procession that would carry John F. Kennedy's coffin from its resting place in the East Room of the White House to the Capitol rotunda. While waiting for the completion of a private Catholic mass in the East Room, network television switched to the police station in Dallas, just in time to capture live footage of Oswald being shot and fatally wounded by Jack Ruby, a local nightclub owner. Within minutes, the focus shifted back to Washington, where the president's coffin was placed atop a gun carriage pulled by six gray horses for the journey down Pennsylvania Avenue. At the Capitol, a Navy band awaited, prepared to announce John Fitzgerald Kennedy's arrival by playing "Hail to the Chief" for him one last time.

Ruby Shoots Oswald

On Sunday morning, TV crews gathered in the basement of Dallas police headquarters, hoping to catch a glimpse of Lee Harvey Oswald as he was led toward a vehicle that would deliver him to the county jail. As a reporter called out to Oswald for a comment, a man darted from the crowd and shot Oswald in the abdomen at point-blank range. The shooter, Jack Ruby, was a "police groupie," whose presence on the scene no one had questioned.

The Camelot Legacy
1963–1968

Jacqueline Kennedy once said that she and Jack were "icebergs." A better description would hardly be possible. The visible part of their personalities was beautiful, even dazzling. But the greater portion of their emotional lives was hidden from view. No one could really map the depths. Jack Kennedy, certainly, was not brought up to be the kind of person who revealed his innermost feelings to others, even those closest to him. It would never have occurred to him to publicly confess his faults; nor would he court sympathy by complaining about his struggles with poor health and chronic pain. Character, as he saw it, consisted of putting up the best possible front. Even when one's feelings were in turmoil, it was important to embody grace and courage. Although he often seemed to lack a steady moral compass in both his personal life and his conduct of foreign policy, Kennedy believed that it was important for a leader to inspire others. His formal speeches reflected his conviction that ideals matter, even if we can't always live up to them. When speaking more personally, he strove for a light touch, displaying a self-deprecating sense of humor that revealed his awareness of the gap between image and reality.

These qualities accounted for Jack Kennedy's charismatic appeal during his lifetime. After his shocking and violent death, they elevated him to the status of a martyred hero. The instant transformation was facilitated by Jackie. Despite the traumatic events in Dallas, within hours of her return to Washington she

was busy researching how the deaths of earlier presidents had been memorialized, especially that of Abraham Lincoln. The funeral rites she planned so meticulously created a sense of historical continuity that helped to calm the nerves of a stunned public. Her dignified demeanor also made a deep impression on millions of television viewers.

At the time of his death, Kennedy's reelection had been far from assured. The threat of a damaging scandal could never be entirely dismissed, and Kennedy's detractors were growing increasingly vocal. Victor Lasky's exposé *JFK: The Man and the Myth* was a best-seller. Lasky withdrew the book after the assassination, and for several years the world seemed to forget that the late president had not always been universally revered. The legend grew that his nearly three years in office had been the era of Camelot—in the words of the title song of the musical of the same name, "one brief shining moment" of heroic glory and romantic innocence.

In truth, some of Kennedy's loyal Democratic supporters had admired him almost despite his stands on the issues. After his death, one often heard the argument that Kennedy had been moving toward more aggressive stands on civil rights and social welfare legislation and away from his view of

A Nation Grieves

Monday, November 25, the day of JFK's funeral, was declared a national day of mourning. One of the most poignant sights that day was three-year-old John F. Kennedy Jr., saluting his father's coffin from the steps of St. Matthew's Cathedral after the funeral mass.

underdeveloped nations as an ideological battleground. Ken O'Donnell, a longtime aide, even claimed that Jack had made up his mind to withdraw American advisors from Vietnam after the 1964 election. Bobby Kennedy, always more emotionally volatile than his older brother, did indeed undergo a dramatic transformation in the mid-1960s. He publicly denounced the Vietnam conflict as immoral and was heard to say more than once that he wished he'd had the experience of being born black and poor. No one can say for sure how Jack's views might have changed had he lived, but it would be hard to imagine him expressing envy of the underprivileged. His sense of irony was too acute.

A growing public appetite for conspiracy theories formed the dark side of the Camelot legend. After Lee Harvey Oswald's capture, it soon became known that he was a mentally unstable loner who labored under the delusion that left-wing Americans would see his action as heroic. But Jackie Kennedy no doubt spoke for millions when she instinctively protested against the explanation that her husband had died at the hands of a "silly little Communist." Many preferred to cling to the instant judgment that right-wing "hate" had killed the president, if only because that theory gave them an enemy on whom they could vent their outrage. Others irrationally blamed the entire city of Dallas or even Lyndon Johnson.

THE RIDERLESS HORSE

The riderless horse, sometimes called a caparisoned horse, is an old military custom practiced in honor of a departed leader. At the funeral of John F. Kennedy, the role was played by a black gelding named Black Jack who walked behind the president's coffin carrying a saddle and sword, with a pair of cavalry boots turned backward in the stirrups. Born at Fort Enid, Oklahoma, Black Jack was named in honor of Gen. John F. ("Black Jack") Pershing, who commanded U.S. troops during World War I. He is often described as a Morgan horse—a large breed favored by mounted police units, for its ability to put the officer high above a crowd. But other sources say Black Jack's breeding is "unknown."

The Monday rituals began with the president's coffin being removed from the Capitol in the presence of a military honor guard. Mrs. Kennedy rode behind the caisson to the White House. There, she left her car and walked to the cathedral at the head of a procession of mourners, including dignitaries from around the world.

Black Jack's appearance at the Kennedy rites made him famous, and he eventually walked in more than 1,000 funerals, including those of three more U.S. presidents—Hoover, Eisenhower, and Johnson. He died in 1976 and was buried on the parade grounds at Fort Meyer, Virginia. In recent years, the saddle and boots used at Kennedy's funeral, as well as other memorabilia, have been on display at the Fort Meyer stables.

Alternative theories about the assassination soon sprang up. Oswald was portrayed as a pawn of the KGB, Castro's security forces, anti-Castro Cubans bitter over the Bay of Pigs fiasco, or Mafia kingpins who felt that the Kennedys were persecuting them despite their best efforts to eliminate Castro. As intriguing and even plausible as such theories might be at first glance, they were based almost entirely on unreliable hearsay and strained conjecture.

Ironically, Jackie and Bobby Kennedy's overzealous attempts to guard Jack's memory eventually caused the first cracks in the Camelot myth. Jackie took exception to Arthur Schlesinger Jr.'s comparison of her late husband to a Roman senator—she thought he had more in common with the ancient Greeks. She turned against Red Fay, nanny Maud Shaw, and her old friend Ben Bradlee because they dared to publish books based on their personal reminiscences. In 1966, she and Bobby became involved in an ugly public wrangle with William Manchester. Manchester had been handpicked by the family to write an authorized account of the assassination, but on the eve of his book's serialization

THE KENNEDY HALF DOLLAR

The portrait of John F. Kennedy used on the half-dollar was designed by Gilroy Roberts, based on an existing image from Kennedy's presidential medal.

Within days of Kennedy's death, Eva Adams, the director of the U.S. Mint, began to consider ways to honor the late president on a coin. A one-dollar Kennedy coin was briefly considered. A Kennedy quarter was ruled out because Mrs. Kennedy did not want her husband's image to displace that of George Washington. Mint officials soon settled on a Kennedy half dollar, but since U.S. coins can be changed only after 25 years, an act of Congress was required to retire the Benjamin Franklin half dollar then in circulation. The first Kennedy half dollar proofs were issued in January 1964 and regular coins became available on March 24. Enormous numbers of 1964 coins were minted, but because Americans tended to regard them as keepsakes, they failed to achieve wide circulation.

in *Look* magazine, Jackie had second thoughts. Her reluctance to see personal details of the tragedy revealed in print was understandable, but the accusation that Manchester had sensationalized his subject was not.

A comment Jackie made to Manchester, when later reported, exposed the public to a side of her that they had never seen. "Anybody who is against me will look like a rat unless I run off with Eddie Fisher," she told him threateningly. Meanwhile, the lawsuit she and Bobby brought in an attempt to halt publication of Manchester's book had the contrary effect of turning details that might have passed without much notice into tidbits of gossip. "Jackie falls off her pedestal," announced gossip columnist Liz Smith at the time.

On June 5, 1968, hours after winning the California Democratic primary, Bobby Kennedy was shot dead by another lone assassin, Sirhan Sirhan. Four months later, Jackie married Greek shipping tycoon Aristotle Onassis, much to the disappointment of those who had idolized her as the grieving widow of a murdered American hero. And in July 1969, Ted Kennedy, who had been elected to the U.S. Senate in 1962, was involved in a controversial automobile accident on the island of Chappaquiddick that took the life of a former Robert Kennedy aide, Mary Jo Kopechne.

Those three events, happening in rapid succession, marked the end of Camelot. Any realistic hope that the aborted presidency of John F. Kennedy would be just the beginning of a family dynasty had been dashed. Rose Kennedy, who had been working to raise money

THE JOHN FITZGERALD KENNEDY LIBRARY

The earliest presidential libraries were modest buildings, established primarily to serve scholars and students. Soon after JFK's death, it became apparent that his library would be far more imposing, also doing duty as a museum and a shrine. Jacqueline Kennedy personally interviewed architects and chose the Shanghai-born Modernist I.M. Pei to design the structure.

Dedicated in 1979, the Kennedy Library featured an imposing triangular white tower overlooking Boston Harbor, and it quickly become one of Pei's most

I. M. Pei's concrete and glass tower stands on a nine-and-one-half–acre park overlooking Boston harbor.

admired designs. The library's effective use of audio-visual exhibits makes it an appealing destination for tourists, who visit at the rate of about 200,000 a year. It has not always been equally popular with scholars. JFK's papers are not covered by the Presidential Records Act of 1978, and the library's policies have generally been the most restrictive of any presidential archive.

to cover Bobby's campaign debts, energetically defended her fourth son, Ted, telling one reporter who was amazed by her self-possession, "How you cope is the important thing—not the events themselves." But for her husband, the Chappaquiddick scandal seemed to be the final blow. Joe declined steadily, stopped eating or wearing the glasses that corrected his rapidly declining eyesight, and was soon essentially paralyzed. He died that November.

By the end of the decade, American culture was in the throes of a revolution. Opinion turned against the Vietnam conflict and, indeed, against the very premise that winning the Cold War was an important mission for American foreign policy. Lyndon Johnson and Richard Nixon bore the brunt of the anti-authoritarian mood that gripped the country, but Jack Kennedy's reputation also suffered posthumously. The mid-1970s saw the emergence in quick succession of devastating revelations about his involvement with Marilyn Monroe, Judith Campbell Exner, Mary Pinchot Meyer, and Dr. Max Jacobson.

DALLAS REMEMBERS

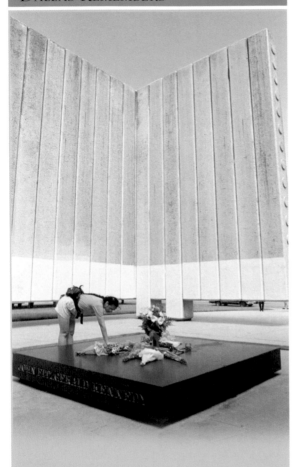

Deciding how to commemorate the assassination of the 35th president of the United States was a painful process for the people of Dallas. The city's John F. Kennedy Memorial, informally called the cenotaph, was designed by world-renowned architect Philip Johnson. By the time it was dedicated in 1970, Johnson's creation had been downgraded from marble to concrete and consigned to a location away from Dealey Plaza, behind the county courthouse. During the 1980s, Dallas was finally ready to discuss the renovation of the Dealey Plaza area, and there was anxious debate over what to name a museum planned for the former Texas School Book Depository building. The result was the Sixth Floor Museum, which opened to the public on the Presidents' Day holiday, 1989.

In 1975, meanwhile, a Senate Select Committee opened an investigation into the CIA and its role in plots to assassinate foreign leaders. The committee focused on allegations that the agency had followed its own agenda, keeping President Kennedy and his successors in the dark about the details of its operations. There followed a spate of books that blamed Kennedy's assassination on rogue CIA agents. Oliver Stone's film *JFK* marked the apotheosis of this viewpoint. Based on the story of Jim Garrison, an eccentric New Orleans district attorney whose theories of the assassination had been discredited years earlier, the film took the position that Jack Kennedy was killed by representatives of the military-industrial complex because he was preparing to withdraw from Vietnam. *JFK* was a work of "faction," a mélange of fact and fiction. Stone never claimed that the elements of his story were accurate, yet somehow filmgoers were expected to find that they illuminated "a higher truth"— that sinister unseen forces manipulate American society from behind a smokescreen of democracy.

It is hard to imagine a viewpoint that would have been more repugnant to the 35th president. Jack Kennedy, who grew up with the knowledge that he would probably die young (thanks to his poor health) despite all his advantages, understood as surely as anyone that life is often unfair. But he also realized that the American political system, with all its flaws, created unparalleled opportunities for individual accomplishment. After all, his own family had begun as famine refugees and rose to the pinnacle of power in a single century.

Kennedy never promised a utopia. His chosen metaphor was the "New Frontier," a place of struggle and sacrifice, and he spent most of his three years in office preoccupied with the challenge of preserving democracy against the threats posed by the cold war. In life, Jack Kennedy personified youth, optimism, and vigor—an image that raised popular expectations that he no doubt would have been hard-pressed to fulfill had he lived. With hindsight, however, he seems to belong more to the world of FDR, Truman, and Eisenhower than to the era of cultural ferment and self-doubt that began with his death.

JFK and the Statue of Liberty, 1960

Photo Credits

Page #/Position	Credit	Page #/Position	Credit	Page #/Position	Credit
1	William Philpott/ Reuters/TimePix	58-60	Courtesy John Fitzgerald Kennedy Library, Boston	110	AP Photo
2-5	Courtesy John Fitzgerald Kennedy Library, Boston	61	AP Photo/William B. Plowman	111	© *New Bedford Standard-Times*
6	AP Photo	62-64	Courtesy John Fitzgerald Kennedy Library, Boston	112	© *Look* Magazine
7	Carl Mydans/TimePix	65	Pix Inc./ TimePix	113	AP Photo
8-9	Hulton Archive/Getty Images	66	International News Photos	114	Bettmann/Corbis
10	Courtesy John Fitzgerald Kennedy Library, Boston	67	Underwood & Underwood/Corbis	115	Courtesy John Fitzgerald Kennedy Library, Boston
11	The Granger Collection, New York	68	Courtesy John Fitzgerald Kennedy Library, Boston	116	Bettmann/Corbis
12	Corbis	69	Hulton Archive/Getty Images	117	Grey Villet/TimePix
13	Courtesy John Fitzgerald Kennedy Library, Boston	70-71	Verner Reed/TimePix	118-121	Bettmann/Corbis
14	Hulton Archive/Getty Images	72	Bettmann/Corbis	122	© *Look* Magazine
15	Courtesy John Fitzgerald Kennedy Library, Boston	73	Yale Joel/TimePix	123	Cecil Stoughton, White House/John Fitzgerald Kennedy Library, Boston
16	© *Look* Magazine	74	© *Look* Magazine	124	Ed Clark/TimePix
17	Courtesy John Fitzgerald Kennedy Library, Boston	75	© *New Bedford Standard-Times*	125-126	Courtesy John Fitzgerald Kennedy Library, Boston
18	© *Boston Herald*	76	AP Photo	127	AP Photo
19-25	Courtesy John Fitzgerald Kennedy Library, Boston	77	John Swope/TimePix	128	Art Shay/TimePix
26	Underwood & Underwood/Corbis	78-79	Courtesy John Fitzgerald Kennedy Library, Boston	129-133	Courtesy John Fitzgerald Kennedy Library, Boston
27	Courtesy John Fitzgerald Kennedy Library, Boston	80-81	© *New Bedford Standard-Times*	134	AP Photo
28	© *New Bedford Standard-Times*	82	Morgan Studios/Getty Images	135	© *Look* Magazine
30	Courtesy John Fitzgerald Kennedy Library, Boston	83	© *New Bedford Standard-Times*	136	Art Rickerby/TimePix
31-32	Hulton Archive/Getty Images	84	Courtesy John Fitzgerald Kennedy Library, Boston	137	AP Photo
33	Courtesy John Fitzgerald Kennedy Library, Boston	85	Hy Peskin/*Life* Magazine, Copyright Time Inc./TimePix	138	© 1967 (Renewed 1995) The Sixth Floor Museum at Dealey Plaza. All Rights Reserved
34	© *New Bedford Standard-Times*	86-87	Lisa Larsen/TimePix	139	AP Photo
35	Courtesy John Fitzgerald Kennedy Library, Boston	88-89	Hulton Archive/Getty Images	140 top	Carl Mydans/TimePix
36-37	Courtesy John Fitzgerald Kennedy Library, Boston	90	AP Photo	140 bott.	DK Media Library
38-39	Corbis	91	© *Look* Magazine	141	Hulton Archive/Getty Images
40	Hulton Archive/Getty Images	92	Corbis	142-143	AP Photo
41-43	Courtesy John Fitzgerald Kennedy Library, Boston	93	Courtesy John Fitzgerald Kennedy Library, Boston	144-145	© *Look* Magazine
44	Marcus Adams	94	Hulton Archive/Getty Images	146	AP Photo
45	Hulton Archive/Getty Images	95	Mark Shaw	147	Courtesy John Fitzgerald Kennedy Library, Boston
46	Hugo Jaeger/TimePix	96	Burton Berinsky	148	Courtesy Hazel Armstead
47-51	Hulton Archive /Getty Images	97	© *Ebony*	149	Allan Goodrich/John Fitzgerald Kennedy Library, Boston
52-53	AP Photo	98-99	Courtesy John Fitzgerald Kennedy Library, Boston	150	AFP/Corbis
54-55	Hulton Archive/Getty Images	100	© *New Bedford Standard-Times*	151	Henry Grossman/TimePix
56	Courtesy John Fitzgerald Kennedy Library, Boston	101	Courtesy John Fitzgerald Kennedy Library, Boston		
57	Bettmann/Corbis	102	AP Photo		
		103	Paul Schutzer/TimePix		
		104	AP Photo		
		105	David J. & Janice L. Frent Collection/Corbis		
		106-109	Courtesy John Fitzgerald Kennedy Library, Boston		

Jacket images:

Front:	Bettmann/Corbis

Back (left to right):

1	Courtesy John Fitzgerald Kennedy Library, Boston
2	Hy Peskin/*LIFE* Magazine @Time Inc./TimePix
3	Bettmann/Corbis
4	Wally McNamee/Corbis
Author photo	© Joyce Milton

Acknowledgements

The publishers would like to thank A&E Networks, Avalon Publishing Group, and their associates for their hard work and good humor throughout this project. Special thanks go to Max Alexander, Tracy Armstead, and Lisa Vaughn for efforts above and beyond the call of duty, and to Sean Moore, f-stop fitzgerald, and Will Balliett for their vision in conceiving this series and their determination to make it a reality. We would also like to extend our continued appreciation to ColourScan Ltd., Singapore, for their excellent work.

Avalon Publishing Group would like to thank Judith McQuown, Jonathan Gregg, and Nanette Cardon for their efforts on this project, as well as the kind cooperation of Hilary Johnston at TimePix, Yvette Reyes at AP Wide World Photo, Colombe Meurin at Photos12.com, and Valerie Zars at Hulton Getty. At DK, Chuck Lang for his support; Chuck Wills for his dogged pursuit of accuracy and good writing; Dirk Kaufman for his great design eye, and Gregor Hall for keeping things moving with patience and understanding. At AETN, Juan Davila, Chey Blake, Charles Wright, Liz Durkin, and David Walmsley all helped put the pieces together, Cindy Berenson kept the ball rolling with her grateful professionalism and, most of all, thanks to Carrie Trimmer, who has supported this series and has contributed to it in so many ways above and beyond the call.

Additional Captions

pg. 1: The Presidential Seal.

pg. 2-3: John Fitzgerald Kennedy during his congressional campaign in Massachusetts.

pg. 4-5: John Fitzgerald Kennedy taking the oath of office.

pg. 8-9: Washington Street in Boston, about 1859.

pg. 24-25: Jack and his brother Ted, summering at the Kennedy compound in Hyannis Port, prepare to set sail.

pg. 38-39: Hungry men line up outside a Depression-era soup kitchen in Chicago operated by Al Capone. The sign reads: FREE SOUP COFFEE & DOUGHNUTS FOR THE UNEMPLOYED.

pg. 52-53: A PT boat on maneuvers in the Pacific on August 1, 1942. The U.S. invasion of the Solomon Islands, beginning later that month, would become the PT fleet's most important mission of the war.

pg. 70-71: Jack campaigns for the Senate in 1952. He was initially considered a lightweight compared to the popular Republican incumbent, Henry Cabot Lodge, Jr.

pg. 88-89: Pro-Kennedy delegates at the 1960 Democratic convention raise the slogan "A Time for Greatness."

pg. 106-107: On Inauguration Day, 1960, JFK calls on Americans to ask what they can do for their country.

pg. 120-121: Union members carrying placards calling for full employment and fair housing join the August 28, 1963 March on Washington.

pg. 132-133: A caisson similar to the one used for the funeral of Abraham Lincoln carries JFK's body through the streets of Washington to St. Matthew's cathedral.

pg. 144-145: Ted, Jack, and Bobby, relaxing together at Hyannis Port. With Jack's death, the mantle of dynastic expectations passed first to Bobby, then to the youngest brother.

Index

A

Acheson, Dean, 129
Addison's disease
 back problems, 36, 41, 65, 66, 67, 91
 childhood illnesses, 25, 35, 36, 37, 41
 diagnosis, 41, 77
 general symptoms, 53, 65, 66, 67, 69
 medications, 41, 77, 81, 100, 123, 140
 public disclosure, 100
 public reaction to appearance, 74, 78
Alcatraz, 136
Algeria, 94, 95
allergies, 43, 83
Amagiri, 61
Amerasia spy scandal, 89, 90
The American Dream, 105
American Jewish Conference, 135
Archbishop of Boston, 20
Arlington National Cemetery, 142, 142
Arvad, Inga, 56–59, 57, 65
assassination, 137–43
asthma, 43
Astor, Lady Nancy, 46
Athenia, 48, 48, 49, 54
atom bombs. See nuclear warfare
Auchincloss, Hugh D., 84, 86
Auchincloss, Jamie, 84

B

back problems, 36, 41, 65, 66, 67, 91
Baker, Bobby, 126
Bartlett, Charlie and Martha, 81–82
Bay of Pigs, 112–14, 117–18, 124, 126
Berlin, 122–23, 133, 142
Bethlehem Steel, 10
Billings, K. LeMoyne "Lem"
 military service, 56, 56
 at school with Kennedy, 36, 36, 40, 41
 trip to Europe with Kennedy, 42, 42, 43
birth control pill, 105
Bissell, Richard, 112, 113, 117
Biuki, 63
Black, Hugo, 128
Black Jack (funeral horse), 147
books
 on the assassination, 148
 ghost-written, 78, 92–93
 love of, 26, 37, 42
 written by Kennedy, 50–51, 69
bootlegging, 26, 29
Boston
 John Fitzgerald Kennedy Library, 108,
 149, 149
 in the 1800s, 8, 9, 14, 14
Bouvier, Jacqueline. See also Kennedy,
 Jacqueline Bouvier

appearance, 84–85
background, 82–85
courtship, 81–82, 83, 85–86
education, 85
love of horses, 83, 83, 84, 84
wedding, 86, 86, 87
Bouvier, Janet Lee, 84, 85, 86, 133
Bouvier, John "Black Jack" Vernour, III, 82,
 82, 84, 85, 86
Bouvier, John Vernour, Jr., 82
Bowen, Lester W., 74
Bradlee, Benjamin, 105, 124, 125, 148
Bradlee, Tony, 126
Bronxville residence, 30
Brookline residence, 26
Bundy, McGeorge, 29
Burkley, Adm. George C., 123, 150

C

"Camelot legacy," 145–50
Campbell, Judith. See Exner, Judith
 Campbell
Cannon, Frances Ann, 54, 65
Canterbury, 36
Cardinal Eugenio Pacelli, 43
Cassini, Igor, 85
Cassini, Oleg, 81, 107, 109
Castro, Fidel, 117
 in conspiracy theories, 148
 during the Cuban missile crisis, 131
 Oswald's admiration of, 141
 plans to overthrow. See Bay of Pigs
Catholicism and Catholics
 divorce, 32
 effects on the presidency, 74, 98, 108
 interfaith marriage, 54, 66
 marital relations, 23
 political views of constituents, 78
 of Rose Kennedy, 20, 23, 32, 54, 66
 segregation of neighborhoods, 9, 14
Cavendish, Billy (Marquess of Hartington),
 45, 54, 66, 67, 69
cenotaph, 150, 150
Central Intelligence Agency (CIA)
 assassination of foreign leaders, 150
 and the Bay of Pigs, 113, 117, 118, 124
 post-missile crisis operations in Cuba,
 134
 Southeast Asia operations, 127
Chamberlain, Neville, 46, 47, 50
Chappaquiddick, 148–49
China, 77
Choate, 36–37, 40, 41
Choiseul, 64
Churchill, Pamela Digby, 77, 77
Churchill, Randolph, 77
Churchill, Sir Winston, 37, 37, 49, 107

Churchill, Winston II, 77
civil rights movement, 125, 128, 134, 135
Clark, Blair, 50
Clay, Cassius, 101
Clay, Gen. Lucius, 122
"Clivenden set," 45–46
Cohn, Roy, 89, 90
coin with Kennedy portrait, 148
Cold War, 76, 77, 108, 112, 118, 149
Columbia Trust Company, 10
Communism. See also Cold War
 global spread in 1961, 112
 McCarthyism, 90
 in Southeast Asia, 127
 on U.S. foreign policy, 94
 World War II, 46
Communist Control Act, 90
Communist Party USA, 90, 141
competitiveness as a family value, 34–36
Conboy, Kikoo (nursemaid), 9
Conklin, Capt. F. L., 64
Connally, Gov. John, 136, 137
Connery, Sean, 118, 118
conspiracy theory of the assassination, 139,
 148, 150
Cuba
 Bay of Pigs, 112–14, 117–18, 124, 126
 missile crisis, 125, 129, 129, 131
 post-missile crisis, 134
Cuban Brigade, 131
Curley, James Michael, 20, 22, 73, 73
Czechoslovakia, 48

D

Daley, Mayor Richard, 105
Davids, Jules, 92
Davis, Mary, 75, 76
Davis, Sir Daniel, 77
de Gaulle, Gen. Charles, 121
Democratic Party
 during McCarthyism, 90
 National Convention of 1956, 98
 role of John F. Kennedy, 76
 role of Joseph P. Kennedy, 39
 role of Patrick J. Kennedy, 13–14
Des Rosiers, Janet, 33
Dickinson, Angie, 110
Diem, Pres. Ngo Dinh, 127, 134
Dirksen, Everett, 134
doll, 61
Donnaly, Eugene P., 135
Donovan, Robert J., 64
draft lottery, 53
Drawdy, Leon, 62
Drewitch, Edmund, 62
drugs. See medications and drugs
Dulles, Allen, 113, 114

E

East Germany, 122–23
Edwards, India, 100
Eichmann, Adolf, 117
Eisenhower, Pres. Dwight, 76, 104, 107, 108, 147
Elizabeth I, Queen of England, 44
Elizabeth II, Queen of England, 45
Eroni, 63
ExCom, 129, 129
Exner, Judith Campbell, 113, 113, 124, 149

F

Falaise, Hank, 31
family values and dynamics, 34–36, 54, 86–87
fascism, 43
Fay, Red
 book of memoirs, 148
 on the Kennedys, 71
 political activities for Kennedy, 73
 relationship with the Kennedys, 69, 110
 Undersecretary of the Navy, 73
Federal Bureau of Investigation (FBI)
 and Arvad, 56, 57, 58, 65
 and Campbell, 124
 loyalty board, 90
 and the Pulitzer Prize, 92
Fejos, Paul, 57, 58
Fenian Council, 12
Fermi, Enrico, 63
Film Booking Office (FBO), 29
films about Kennedy, 150
films narrated by Kennedy, 93, 98
Fitzgerald, Eunice (aunt), 17
Fitzgerald, Fred (uncle), 17
Fitzgerald, James, 14–15
Fitzgerald, John Francis, Jr. (uncle), 17, 19
Fitzgerald, John Francis "Honey Fitz"
 (grandfather)
 childhood, 14, 15
 education and jobs, 15
 on Joe Kennedy, 20, 23, 31
 on Kathleen Kennedy's marriage, 66
 personality, 11, 15, 16, 18
 political career, 15, 16, 16, 17, 22
 support of Kennedy in politics, 72, 73
 "Toodles" affair, 20, 22, 32, 73
Fitzgerald, Josie Hannon (grandmother), 17, 17, 18, 20
Fitzgerald, Mary Agnes (aunt), 17, 18, 27, 123
Fitzgerald, Rosanna (great-grandmother), 14–15, 108
Fitzgerald, Rose Elizabeth (mother). See
 also Kennedy, Rose Fitzgerald
 childhood, 10, 17, 17–18, 19
 education, 18, 20
 and Joseph Patrick, 18, 20, 20, 22
 personal style, 10, 18, 44

Fitzgerald, Thomas (great-grandfather), 14, 108
Fitzgerald, Thomas (uncle), 17
Fleming, Ian, 118
foreign policy
 Bay of Pigs, 112–14, 117–18, 124, 126
 Cold War, 76, 77, 108, 112, 118, 149
 Vietnam conflict, 126–27, 134, 136, 146, 149
Fox, John, 80
Freedom Riders, 128
Freeman, Arthur, 79
funeral, 132–33, 143, 146, 146, 147, 147

G

Gargan, Ann, 123, 123
Georgetown residence, 95, 96
George VI, King of England, 44
Germany. See also East Germany; West
 Germany
 Kennedy in, 43, 48
 pre-WWII, 43, 46
 WWII, 49, 67, 68
G.I. Jack action figure, 61
Giancana, Sam, 94, 113, 116, 124, 124
Glenn, Lt. Col. John H., Jr., 125, 125
Glen Ora residence, 124
Goldwater, Barry, 94
golf, 33, 100, 100
gravesite, 142, 142
Great Britain
 Joe Kennedy Jr. in London embassy, 47, 47, 49
 John F. Kennedy visit to, 43
 Joseph P. Kennedy as ambassador, 43–47, 44, 46, 47, 49, 51, 67, 67
 pre-WWII, 46
 WWII, 49, 68
Great Depression, 38–39, 39
Greer, Bill, 137
Gunboat No. 1, 64

H

half dollar coin, 148
Hammersmith Farm, 83, 83, 86, 95
Harriman, Averell, 72, 77
Harris, Charles, 61, 62
Hartington, Marchioness. See Kennedy,
 Kathleen "Kick"
Hartington, Marquess of, 45, 54, 66, 67, 69
Harvard University
 consultants from, 78
 Crimson, 41, 49, 50
 Joe Kennedy Jr. in, 41, 42, 43, 47
 John F. Kennedy in, 41, 42, 43, 49–50, 74
 Joseph P. Kennedy in, 11
 LSD at, 125
health aspects
 Addison's disease. See Addison's
 disease
 allergies, 43, 83

asthma, 43
 back problems, 36, 41, 65, 66, 67, 91
 Joseph Kennedy, stroke, 123
 and military service, 53, 54, 59, 65
 Rosemary Kennedy
 lobotomy, 55–56
 mental retardation, 22, 23, 25–26, 32, 55
 scarlet fever, 25
Hemingway, Ernest, 114
Henie, Sonja, 80
Hersey, John, 54, 65, 65
Hickory Hill residence, 96, 96
Hiss, Alger, 90
Hitler, Adolf, 46
Hoffa, Jimmy, 80, 94, 94, 96
Hoover, J. Edgar, 57, 65, 124, 134
Hoover, Pres. Herbert, 147
Hull, Cordell, 47
Humphrey, Hubert H., 90, 97–98, 100
Hungary, 94
Husted, John, 85
Hyannis Port Kennedy Compound
 daily life, 34
 family reunions and summers, 30, 30, 31
 Gloria Swanson at, 31
 golf, 100, 100
 grounds, 28, 28
 Jacqueline Kennedy at, 81, 85
 news of Joe Jr.'s death, 67
 purchase of property, 28
 Rose Kennedy at, 33

I

Inauguration Day of 1961, 106–7, 107–8
Ireland, Kennedy visit to, 77
Irish immigrants, 11, 11–12, 14
 "lace curtain" or "high," 9, 19
 prejudice against, 12, 12, 29
Italy, 43

J

Jacobson, Dr. Max, 101, 123, 128, 149
Japan, 60–61, 63, 64
JFK, 150
John F. Kennedy Memorial, 150, 150
John Fitzgerald Kennedy Library, 108, 149, 149
Johnson, Lyndon
 during Berlin crisis, 122
 campaign, 97, 100
 funeral, 147
 and the March on Washington, 135
 as vice president, 101
Johnson, Philip, 150
Johnston, William, 62
Jordan, Dr. Sara, 91
Joseph P. Kennedy, Jr. Foundation, 55
journalism, 72, 82

K

Kane, Joe, 73
Kennedy, Bridget (great-grandmother), 12
Kennedy, Caroline (daughter), 94, 95, 96, 111
Kennedy, Edward (brother), 32
Kennedy, Ethel (sister-in-law), 28, 85
Kennedy, Eunice (sister), 27, 30, 78. See also Shriver, Eunice Kennedy
 birth, 26
 and Joe McCarthy, 89
 and John's death, 143
 political activities, 78, 80
Kennedy, Jacqueline Bouvier (wife)
 during the assassination, 137, 140
 at the funeral, 146, 147
 marriage, 87, 89, 95, 96
 miscarriages, 87, 95
 personal style, 107, 109, 109, 110–11, 112, 121
 political activities, 98, 100, 104
 role as first lady, 108, 110–11, 136, 146
 role as wife, 86–87, 95, 108, 110
 sailing, 35
Kennedy, Jean (sister), 30, 78
 birth, 30
 family dynamics, 33, 35
 political activities, 78, 80
Kennedy, Joe Patrick, Jr. (brother), 30
 book as memorial to, 69
 childhood, 10, 11, 22, 22, 23, 26–27, 29, 36
 death, 67, 68, 69
 education, 26, 29, 31, 36, 40–41
 in London embassy, 47, 47, 49
 military service, 53, 68, 68, 69
 personality, 26, 29, 40
Kennedy, John F., Jr. (son), 108, 111, 112, 146
Kennedy, John "Jack" Fitzgerald
 birth, 9, 108
 early childhood, 11, 22, 22, 23
 education, 26, 29, 36–37, 40–42, 43, 49–50
 military service
 Office of Naval Intelligence, 53–54, 56
 PT-boat service, 52–53, 58–59, 59–65, 60, 66, 69
 courtship and wedding, 81–82, 83, 85–87, 86, 87
 presidential campaign, 88–89, 93, 96–102, 99, 103, 103, 105
 Bay of Pigs, 112–14, 117–18, 124, 126
 Cuban missile crisis, 125, 129, 129, 131
 assassination, 137–43
 funeral, 132–33, 143, 146, 146, 147, 147
 admiration of Churchill, 37, 49, 107
 affairs
 Ellen Rometsch, 126, 134
 Gene Tierney, 81

Inga Arvad, 56–59, 57, 65
 Judith Campbell Exner, 113, 113, 124, 149
 Marilyn Monroe, 130, 130, 149
 Mary Pinchot Meyer, 126, 126, 149
 Pamela Turnure, 124
 "Pooh," 96
 Suzy Chang, 124
 Tempest Storm, 87
 appearance, 74, 78, 103, 104
 as a husband, 95
 ignorance on money matters, 54–55, 75
 as a parent, 96, 111
 personality, 26, 29, 37, 42, 57, 59, 74, 145
 relationship with father, 42, 50, 51, 71, 78, 80
 relationship with grandfather, 16
 as replacement for Joe, Jr., 69, 71
 scrimshaw collection, 93, 93
 sense of humor, 59–60, 145
 trips to Europe, 42, 42, 43, 47–49, 76
Kennedy, Joseph Patrick (father), 30
 affairs, 29, 30–31, 32–33, 81
 ambassador to Great Britain, 43–47, 44, 44, 46, 51, 67, 67
 anti-Semitism, 46–47, 51
 appearance, 13, 13, 18
 athletic skills, 18, 20, 20
 business dealings, 10–11, 22, 26, 29, 39, 40, 94
 childhood and education, 13, 18, 19
 death, 149
 on Eleanor Roosevelt, 51
 and Jacqueline, 85
 and John, 39–51, 42, 50, 71, 78, 80
 on Kathleen's marriage, 66
 as a parent, 23, 27, 34, 37, 54, 55, 71
 political activities
 to support John, 73, 78, 80, 97
 to support McCarthy, 89
 to support Roosevelt, 39, 51
 promotion of PT-109, 65–66
 reaction to Joe, Jr.'s death, 67
 reaction to John's death, 143
 and Rose, 18, 20, 20, 22, 23, 31, 33
 social aspirations, 11, 29, 31, 44, 45
 stroke, 123
 wedding, 13, 18, 20, 22
Kennedy, Kathleen (niece), 89
Kennedy, Kathleen "Kick" (sister)
 childhood and adolescence, 25, 27, 30, 40
 death of husband, 69
 marriage to Hartington, 66, 66–67
 personality, 45, 54
 and Peter Milton, 76–77, 78, 79
 presentation at court, 44, 44
 relationship with the family, 54, 69
 success in London society, 45, 45
 volunteer with Red Cross, 60, 66, 69, 79

Kennedy, Mary Augusta Hickey (grandmother), 12–13
Kennedy, Patricia (sister), 27, 30, 78
 marriage to Peter Lawford, 116
 political activities, 78, 80
Kennedy, Patrick (great-grandfather), 11, 12
Kennedy, Patrick Bouvier (son), 133
Kennedy, Patrick Joseph (grandfather), 19
 businesses, 12, 13, 14
 political career, 13–14
Kennedy, Robert Francis "Bobby" (brother), 30, 80
 assassination, 148
 birth, 29
 childhood, 34
 McClellan committee, 80, 94
 political activities
 after Kennedy's death, 146
 for John F., 80, 96, 101
 for McCarthy, 89
 purchase of Hickory Hill, 96
 purchase of the Kennedy Compound, 28
 role in the Kennedy administration, 108, 116, 117, 118, 146
Kennedy, Rose Fitzgerald (mother), 30, 33
 organizational skills, 10, 23, 23
 as a parent, 23, 33, 37, 54, 56
 personality, 33
 political activities, 74, 74, 148–49
 prior to marriage. See Fitzgerald, Rose Elizabeth
 reaction to John's death, 143
 religious beliefs, 20, 23, 32, 54, 66
 response to husband's affairs, 31–32, 33
 withdrawal from the world, 33, 56, 123
Kennedy, Rosemary (sister), 55
 childhood, 22, 22, 23, 25–26, 27, 30, 32
 lobotomy, 55–56
 mental retardation, 22, 23, 25–26, 32, 55
 presentation at court, 44, 44, 45, 55
 at St. Coletta's School, 55, 56
Kennedy, Ted (brother), 31, 80, 143, 148–49
Kennedy Compound. See Hyannis Port Kennedy Compound
Kerr, Jean, 89
Khrushchev, Prem. Nikita
 and the Cuban missile crisis, 129, 131
 meeting with Kennedy in Vienna, 121, 122, 122
 Nixon on, 112
King, Coretta Scott, 128
King, Martin Luther, Jr., 97, 125, 128, 135
King, Martin Luther, Sr., 97
Kirksey, Andrew, 62, 62, 64, 66
Kopechne, Mary Jo, 148
Kowal, Maurice, 62
Krock, Arthur, 50, 56, 85, 92

L

labor reform, 94, 120–21, 127–28
Landis, James, 78
Laos, 127
Laski, Harold, 41, 51
Lawford, Peter, 116, 130
Leary, Timothy, 126
Lee, James T., 82
Lehman, Herbert, 95
Lewis, John, 135
Liberator aircraft, 68
Lincoln, Evelyn, 124
Lindbergh, Anne Morrow, 111
Lindbergh, Charles, 46, 111
lobotomy, 55–56
Lodge, Henry Cabot, Jr., 80
Lord Fitzwilliam, 76–77, 78, 79
LSD, 125, 126
Luce, Clare Boothe, 60, 101
Luce, Henry, 50

M

MacArthur, Gen. Douglas, 60
Macdonald, Torbert
 and Arvad, 57
 as coach, 41
 in Europe with Kennedy, 47, 48
 PT-boat service, 58
 in South Vietnam, 134
 writing by, 50
Macmillan, Harold, 112
Maguire, John, 61, 62, 62
Maine
 Old Orchard Beach, 18, 19, 19
 Poland Springs, 25
Manchester, William, 148
Mansfield, Mike, 134
Mao Tse-tung, 77
March on Washington for Jobs and
 Freedom, 134, 135
Marney, Harold, 62
Massachusetts. See Boston; Hyannis Port
 Kennedy Compound
Mauer, Edmon Edgar, 61, 62, 62
Mayo Clinic, 37
McCarthy, Sen. Joseph
 anti-communist activities, 90
 censure, 90–91
 relationship to Kennedy family, 80, 89
McClellan Rackets Committee, 80, 94
McMahon, Pappy, 61, 62
Meany, George, 94
medications and drugs, 41, 77, 81, 100, 123,
 140
mental retardation, 22, 23, 25–26, 32, 55
Meredith, James, 128, 128
Meyer, Mary Pinchot, 126, 126, 149
military career
 Office of Naval Intelligence, 53–54, 56
 PT-boat service, 52–53, 58–59, 59–65,
 60, 66, 69

Milton, Peter (Lord Fitzwilliam), 76–77, 78,
 79
minimum wage, 76, 127, 128
mobsters, 94, 113, 116, 117, 124, 136
Monroe, Marilyn, 130, 130, 149
Moore, Edward, 31, 49
Morse, Wayne, 90
Muhammed Ali, 100
Mulkern, Patsy, 73
Mussolini, Benito, 43

N

National Council of Churches, 135
Nazis. See also World War II
 and Arvad, 56–57
 Joseph Kennedy on, 46
 pre-WWII, 46, 48, 50
 war crimes, 117
New Frontier theme, 104–5, 107, 150
Nhu, Ngo Dinh, 134
Nixon, Richard M., 76
 "Checkers Speech," 101
 political career, 76
 presidential campaign, 97, 102, 102,
 103, 103
 public perception of, 101, 105
 relationship with Kennedy, 76
North Atlantic Treaty Organization
 (NATO), 131
nuclear warfare, 63, 77, 122, 133, 136. See
 also Cold War; Cuba, missile crisis

O

O'Brien, Larry, 96, 102
O'Donnell, Ken, 73, 96, 146
Olmsted, Frederick Law, 83
Onassis, Aristotle, 133–34, 134, 148
Organization of American States, 114, 131
Oswald, Lee Harvey, 141, 141, 143, 143, 146,
 148
Oxford riots, 128–29

P

Peace Corps, 115
Pei, I.M., 149
Pershing, Gen. John F. "Black Jack," 147
Pinchot, Ruth, 126
Planned Parenthood, 105
Poland, 49, 94
political career
 House of Representatives, 16, 70–71,
 74–78, 85
 Senate, 16, 70–71, 80, 85
presidential campaign, 88–89, 93, 96–102,
 99, 103, 103, 105
 inauguration as president, 106–7,
 107–8
presidency during 1961, 107–18
presidency during 1962, 121–31
presidency during 1963, 133–37
 re-election campaign, 136, 136–37
"Pooh," 96

Pope Pius XII, 43
Powell, Adam Clayton, 100
Powers, Dave, 35
prejudice and discrimination
 anti-Semitism, 46–47
 against a Catholic president, 98
 against the Irish, 12, 12, 29
President's Fitness Award, 55
Prinz, Joachim, 135
Profiles in Courage, 92–93
Profumo, John, 124
Prohibition, 26, 26, 40
Protestants
 Brookline neighborhoods, 9
 Church of England, 45
 conflict with the Catholics in New
 York, 12
 interfaith marriage, 54, 66
PT-59, 60
PT-109 (book by Donovan), 64
PT-109 (patrol boat), 61–64, 65
PT-109 (*Reader's Digest* condensed version),
 65–66
PT-boat service, 52–53, 58–59, 59–65, 60
Pulitzer Prize, 92
The Pursuit of Happiness, 93, 98

R

Rabaul, 61
Randolph, A. Philip, 135
Red Cross, 60, 66, 69, 79
Reuther, Walter, 94, 135
RKO, 29
rocking chairs, 91, 91
Rometsch, Ellen, 126, 134
Roosevelt, Eleanor, 51, 93, 100
Roosevelt, Franklin, Jr., 134
Roosevelt, James, 40
Roosevelt, Pres. Franklin Delano
 Amerasia spy scandal, 89, 90
 and Joseph P. Kennedy, 39, 40, 43, 47,
 67, 67
 during WWII, 49, 89
Ross, Barney, 63
Ruby, Jack, 141, 143, 143
Rusk, Dean, 131, 133
Russo, Joe, 73

S

Sacred Heart Convent, 20, 55
Saigon, 136
sailing, 34, 35, 35, 37, 59, 81, 85
St. Coletta's School, 55, 56
Saltonstall, Leverett, Jr., 29
scarlet fever, 25
Schine, G. David, 90
Schlesinger, Arthur, Jr., 105, 148
Scotland, Kennedy visit to, 43, 48, 49
Securities and Exchange Commission, 40
Shaw, Maud, 148
Shriver, Eunice Kennedy (sister), 55
Shriver, R. Sargent, 55, 80, 115

Sinatra, Frank, 107, 113, 116, 116, 124
Sirhan, Sirhan, 148
Smathers, George, 95
Smith, Maud (nanny), 98
Smith, Stephen, 96
socialism, 41
social revolution, 149, 150
Social Security, 76
Solomon Islands, 60–65
Somerset Importers, 40
Sorensen, Ted
 on the campaign trail, 93–94
 on Kennedy, 98, 128
 speechwriting, 90, 93, 105, 107
 writing on *Profiles in Courage,* 92
Southeast Asia, 126–27
Soviet Union. See also Cold War
 and the Cuban missile crisis, 129, 131
 "missile gap," 102
 nuclear test ban treaty, 133, 136
space exploration, 112
support of Cuba, 113
space exploration, 112, 125, 125
Spain, 42–43
Special Olympics, 55
speechwriting, 76, 90, 93, 105, 107
sports, 34, 34, 35, 37, 41, 59, 81, 85, 100
Stanford University, 53
Starkey, Ray, 61
Stevenson, Adlai, 72, 93, 95, 100, 117, 136
stock market, 128
Storm, Tempest, 87
Student Non-Violent Coordinating
 Committee, 135
Sutton, Billy, 73, 75
Swanson, Gloria, 30–31, 31, 32
Symington, Stuart, 97

T

Tague, Peter, 73
Taylor, George, 74
Thom, Lennie, 62, 65
Tierney, Gene, 81
"Toodles" affair, 20, 22, 32, 73
Townshend, Peter, 79
Travell, Dr. Janet, 91, 108, 123
Truman, Pres. Harry S, 89, 100
Turkey, 131
Turnure, Pamela, 124

U

United Nations, 72, 117
University of Mississippi, 128–29
U.S. Army
 McCarthy investigation of, 90
 Oxford riots, 128–29
U.S. Congress
 John F. Kennedy in, 16, 74–78, 80, 85
 John "Honey Fitz" Fitzgerald in, 15, 22
U.S. Navy
 Joe Kennedy Jr. in, 53, 67, 68, 68–69,
 69
 John F. Kennedy in, 53–54, 56, 56,
 61–64, 65, 69
 Lem Billings in, 56, 56
 Naval Reserves, 53
 Office of Naval Intelligence, 54, 56
 Sixth Naval District Headquarters, 57

V

Victura, 35, 35
Vidal, Gore, 84
Vietnam conflict, 127, 134, 136, 146, 149
Von Dirksen, Herbert, 46
von Stroheim, Erich, 32

W

Watts, James W., 55
Wessel, Horst, 48
West Germany, 122–23, 144
White, Byron "Whizzer," 48
White House
 Oval Office, 112
 state dinners, 111
 television tour, 110, 110
Why England Slept, 50–51, 114
Wilkins, Roy, 135
Willy, Wilford J., 68
 world affairs, early interest in, 35, 37,
 42, 49
World War II
 declaration, 49
 Great Britain during, 49, 68
 role of PT-boats, 60
 U.S. during, 49, 89
writing. See books; journalism;
 speechwriting

Y

Young, Whitney, 135

Z

Zapruder, Abraham, 139
"Zoot-Suit Black," 68

Select Bibliography

Blair, Joan and Clay, Jr. *The Search for JFK.* (Putnam Publishing Group, New York: 1976).

Blight, James G. and Peter Kornbluh, eds. *Politics of Illusion: The Bay of Pigs Invasion Reexamined.* (Lynne Rienner Publishers, Boulder: 1998).

Bradford, Sarah. *America's Queen: The Life of Jacqueline Kennedy Onassis.* (Penguin, New York: 2000).

Bradlee, Benjamin C. *Conversations with Kennedy.* (W. W. Norton & Co., New York: 1975).

Bulkley, Robert J., Jr., *At Close Quarters: PT Boats in the United States Navy.* (Naval Institute Press, Washington, D. C.: 1962).

Cameron, Gail. *Rose: A Biography of Rose Fitzgerald Kennedy.* (Pocket Books, New York: 1971).

Claflin, Edward B. *JFK Wants To Know: Memos from the President's Office, 1961-1963.* (William Morrow & Co., New York: 1991).

Collier, Peter and David Horowitz. *The Kennedys: An American Drama.* (Summit Books, New York: 1984).

Corry, John. *The Manchester Affair.* (Putnam, New York: 1967).

Cutler, John Henry. *"Honey Fitz": Three Steps to the White House.* (Bobbs-Merrill, Indianapolis, 1962).

Exner, Judith. *My Story.* (Grove Press, New York: 1977).

Fay, Paul B., Jr. *The Pleasure of His Company.* (Harper & Row, New York: 1966).

Goodwin, Doris Kearns. *The Fitzgeralds and the Kennedys.* (Simon & Schuster, New York: 1987).

Hamilton, Nigel. *Reckless Youth.* (Random House, New York: 1991).

Herman, Arthur. *Joseph McCarthy: Reexamining the Life and Legacy of America's Most Hated Senator.* (Free Press, New York: 2000).

Hersh, Seymour M. *The Dark Side of Camelot.* (Little, Brown & Co., Boston: 1997).

Heymann, C. David. *A Woman Named Jackie.* (Lyle Stuart, New York: 1989).

Hunt, Conover. *JFK For a New Generation.* (Southern Methodist University Press, Dallas: 1996).

Kennedy, John F. *Profiles in Courage.* (Harper & Row, New York: 1956).

Kennedy, John F. *Prelude to Leadership: The Post-War Diary of John F. Kennedy.* (Regnery Publishing, Inc., Washington, D.C.: 1995).

Kennedy, Rose Fitzgerald. *Times to Remember.* (Doubleday, New York: 1974.)

Joyce Milton

Kenney, Charles. *John F. Kennedy, The Presidential Portfolio: History As Told Though the Collection of the John F. Kennedy Library and Museum.* (Public Affairs, New York: 2000).

Kessler, Ronald. *The Sins of the Father: Joseph P. Kennedy and the Dynasty He Founded.* (Warner Books, New York: 1996).

Kornbluh, Peter, ed. *Bay of Pigs Declassified: The Secret CIA Report on the Invasion of Cuba.* (New Press, New York: 1998).

Lincoln, Evelyn. *My Twelve Years with John F. Kennedy.* (David McKay Co., New York: 1965).

Manchester, William. *Controversy and Other Essays In Journalism.* (Little, Brown & Co., Boston: 1976).

Manchester, William. *The Death of a President: November 1963.* (Harper & Row, New York: 1967).

McTaggart, Lynn. *Kathleen Kennedy: Her Life and Times.* (Doubleday, Garden City, New York: 1983).

Miller, Kerby A. *Emigrants and Exiles: Ireland and the Irish Exodus to North America.* (Oxford University Press, New York: 1985).

Mulvaney, Jay. *Jackie: The Clothes of Camelot.* (St. Martin's Press, New York: 2001).

Nixon, Richard. *RN: The Memoirs of Richard Nixon.* (Grosset & Dunlap, New York: 1978).

O'Donnell, Kenneth P. and David F. Powers. *"Johnny We Hardly Knew Ye": Memories of John Fitzgerald Kennedy.* (Little, Brown & Co., Boston: 1970).

Parmet, Herbert S. *Jack: The Struggles of John F. Kennedy.* (Doubleday, New York: 1980).

Parmet, Herbert S. *JFK: The Presidency of John F. Kennedy.* (Doubleday, New York: 1983).

Posner, Gerald. *Case Closed: Lee Harvey Oswald and the Assassination of JFK.* (Random House, New York: 1993).

Reeves, Richard. *President Kennedy: Profile of Power.* (Simon & Schuster, New York: 1993).

Reeves, Thomas C. *A Question of Character: A Life of John F. Kennedy.* (Free Press, New York: 1991).

Schlesinger, Arthur, Jr. *A Thousand Days: John F. Kennedy in the White House.* (Houghton Mifflin, Boston: 1965).

Searls, Hank. *The Lost Prince: Young Joe, The Forgotten Kennedy.* (World Pub. Co., New York: 1969).

Smith, Amanda, ed. *Hostage to Fortune: The Letters of Joseph P. Kennedy.* (Viking Press, New York: 2001).

Sorensen, Theodore C. *Kennedy.* (Harper & Row, New York: 1965).

Swanson, Gloria. *Swanson on Swanson.* (Random House, New York: 1980).

Tierney, Gene. *Self-Portrait.* (Wyden Books, New York: 1979).

Whelan, Richard. *The Founding Father: The Story of Joseph P. Kennedy.* (New American Library, New York: 1966).